I Didn't Work
This Hard Just To
Get Married

APR 09

CH

I Didn't Work This Hard Just To Get Married

Successful Single
Black Women Speak Out

Nika C. Beamon

Foreword by Dr. Bella DePaulo

Lawrence Hill Books

Library of Congress Cataloging-in-Publication Data
Beamon, Nika C.
  I didn't work this hard just to get married : successful single black
women speak out / Nika C. Beamon.
      p. cm.
  ISBN 978-1-55652-819-4
  1. Single women—United States. 2. African American single people—Psychology. 3. African American women—Psychology. 4. Single
mothers—United States—Psychology. I. Title.
  HQ800.2.B42 2009
  306.81'53092396073—dc22

                              2008050176

Cover design: Rachel McClain
Cover photographs: © Alamy/Corbis
Interior design: Jonathan Hahn
Author photo: AriTaurus420 Photography

© 2009 by Nika C. Beamon
Foreword © 2009 by Dr. Bella DePaulo
All rights reserved
Published by Lawrence Hill Books
An imprint of Chicago Review Press, Incorporated
814 North Franklin Street
Chicago, Illinois 60610
ISBN 978-1-55652-819-4
Printed in the United States of America
5 4 3 2 1

This book is dedicated to:

The women in my life who've shown me the joys of being loved, how it
feels to be loved, and how to choose the right man to love.

The men in my life who've taught me how to fall in love,
how to survive losing love, and how to love myself before
looking for someone to love.

My God for loving me even when I found it hard to love myself.

Contents

Part Six
Divinely Single

Part Seven
Musings on Single Life

Foreword

There are so many reasons to love Nika Beamon's stories about single black women defying expectations. The women who are the stars of this show are inspirational.

Name a stereotype—of women, of African Americans, of single people, or any combination of the above—and there are people in these pages who have shattered it. They live at the intersection of three sets of prejudices—sexism, racism, and singlism—but there is not a victim among them.

My passion is reading and writing and learning about the lives of people who are single. I gather just about everything I can find on the topic—scientific research, media accounts, and life stories as described by the people who are living them—but there has long been a hole in my collection. Until this book came along, the voice of today's successful single black woman was mostly missing.

The statistics have been out there for a while, and they are familiar. For example, the rate of marriage is lower for blacks than for whites, and the rate of single parenting is higher. But it is a different matter entirely to know that many black women are single than to know what that means emotionally, practically, and psychologically. *I Didn't Work This Hard Just to Get Married* invites us into the personal worlds of these women. Some you may already know, either by name or from their work. Others you will be meeting for the first time. I think you will find all of them memorable.

The stories in this book stand on their own as good reading and an entrée into the lives and minds of accomplished single, black, American women. At this historical and sociological moment, though, they are particularly important.

The demographic face of the nation has been steadily changing since the 1950s. Now, at the beginning of the twenty-first century, America in black and white, single and married, looks dramatically different than it did before.

The nuclear family, so steeped in sentiment, once commanded the power of numbers. Now, however, there are fewer households comprising mom, dad, and the kids than of single adults living alone.

The age at which adults first marry (for those who do marry) hit a low in the mid-1950s and has risen steadily ever since. First-time brides and grooms are not so young anymore. The rate of divorce is no longer climbing, but it is still high. Compared with past times, fewer people who divorce go on to remarry; those who do remarry wait longer to do so. Women, especially, are less inclined than they once were to remarry, or to remarry quickly. Women continue to outlive men, so later in life there are many unmarried women.

All of these trends add up to a startlingly new fact of life—Americans (especially women) now spend more years of their adult lives unmarried than married. Living single was once considered transitional—single people marked time until they found "The One." Now it is often marriage that is transitional, connecting one unmarried period of life to another—and only for those who do marry.

Stunning changes have also occurred in the practical importance of marriage, particularly for women. As job opportunities have opened for women over the past decades, many women no longer need a husband for financial security. Some can support themselves, and even a few children, on their own income.

The Food and Drug Administration did not approve the Pill as a safe and effective form of birth control until 1960. Sex outside of marriage was regarded as shameful back then, and having children outside of marriage was more stigmatized than it is now. So, to have sex and children without stigma or shame, women needed to marry. Now, with modern birth control, women can have sex without having children. With modern reproductive science, they can have children without having sex. Marriage is not necessary for any of it.

Successful black women, such as the ones whose stories are told in these pages, are living their lives fully. Many of them are buying homes, traveling, pursuing their passions, and accomplishing great things.

So what's the problem? Why are we so drawn to the stories of people who are single, and why are the lives of today's single people so important historically?

I think it is because our society's view of single people has not caught up with the reality of their lives. As Nika Beamon puts it in her introduction, single black women are defying expectations. The word "expectations" is key. Even though it is utterly ordinary to be single (and in fact, as I've noted, it is the way we spend the better part of our adult lives), living single is still not viewed as ordinary. By a certain age we are all "expected" to be married.

The marriage expectations are not conveyed subtly. Singles get pelted with the "when are you going to get married" question by parents, other relatives, neighbors, and complete strangers. Matrimania, the over-the-top hyping of marriage and weddings, seems to have swept the nation. Movies, television shows, magazines, newspapers, and advertisers cannot seem to get enough of weddings and brides.

What our society is peddling is the myth that single people can never be truly happy and can never lead a genuinely meaningful life. Single women with fabulous jobs are taunted with the insinuation that their jobs won't love them back. They are sternly warned that if they do not hurry and have children, their eggs will dry up. Despite the number of single moms who raise wonderful children, headlines proclaim the (mythical) dire fate that awaits children raised by just one parent.

I call these claims myths because just about all of them are grossly exaggerated or just plain false. I have read stacks of scientific studies, and every one of them shows that single people, on average, are clearly on the happy end of the scale. Getting married results in only a brief blip in happiness around the time of the wedding, then the married people go back to being as happy or as unhappy as they were when they were single. Even the small honeymoon effect is not enjoyed by all newlyweds. People who marry but who will eventually divorce are already becoming less happy, not more so, as their wedding day approaches.

The perils of single parenting are also overblown. One of the reasons is that single parents are rarely raising their children single-handedly. Instead, single moms often have friends and family who have been in their lives for years and who are meaningfully involved in the lives of their children.

The good news about single people and their children is not what we hear in the media or in our cultural conversations. So singles, such as the successful single black women of this book, deal not just with the challenges of creating a life outside of the marital box, they also face the weight of other people's expectations that they belong in that box.

Anyone who thinks that single black women can be kept in a box should read *I Didn't Work This Hard Just to Get Married*. So should everyone else.

—Bella DePaulo, author of *Singled Out: How Singles Are Stereotyped,*
Stigmatized, and Ignored, and Still Live Happily Ever After

Acknowledgments

First let me say this book would not have been possible if not for the generosity of the women featured within who were kind enough to open up their lives and share them with me and the world. To them I say a humble thank you: Kim Coles, Deborah Gregory, Susan Chapman, Jackie DeVaughn, Pamela Harris, Lisa Parker, Shenequa Grey, Effie T. Brown, Nancey Flowers, Sheila Bridges, JC Lamkin, Capt. Gwyneth Bradshaw, Lacy Lewis, Camille Young, Sidney Morris.

Additionally I must say a special thanks to my personal friends, Kiada Moragne and Catherine McKenzie. You two not only supported my aspiration to write this book, but also strengthened our bond by taking the extra step of becoming part of it.

My gratitude must also be extended to the three bright, talented women who were kind enough to read the book in its raw form and provide advance praise: Terrie Williams, Abiola Abrams, and Nicky Grist. I am also appreciative of the time Dr. Julianne Malveaux, Pat Stevenson, and Carol Taylor spent on my manuscript.

Recognition must be given to Bella DePaulo, who was a stranger to me before this project but whom I now consider a friend. You agreed to write the foreword for this book based on the premise alone. I am honored by your bigheartedness.

Of course no one would be reading my words or these women's stories if not for the vision of my editor Susan Betz at Lawrence Hill

Books. Fate allowed me to pick up a trade magazine that described her move to the imprint just as I was ready to give up on ever finding a publisher for this project. As luck would have it, she was not only the right editor for the project, but has also turned out to be one of my greatest champions.

I would also like to extend a special thanks to Kenon Lee, James Black, Kamia Funchess, Diane Elliott, Ilene Rosen, Alexia Quinzon, Alexis Keim, Daisy Jackson, Donald and Ana Lyons, Karen Murphy, Lakiesha Bostick, Lisa Brown, Matthew Harrington, Ralph Rogers, Bill King, Sandra Bookman, Kemberly Richardson, Sixto Reynoso, Tanya Mills, Tori Bramble Gasmalla, Ceylone Boothe, Warren Fludd, and all of my coworkers at WABC-TV.

I must say, I wouldn't be half the woman I am today if not for the undying love and support of my parents Randolph and Gloria, my brothers Taharka and Randy.

Finally, to Branden Cobb, I say thank you for teaching me the depth of love, forgiveness, understanding, and acceptance.

Bless you all.

Introduction

Single and Defying Expectations

Expectation is defined as something that is probable or most likely to happen. It is also described as something we are bound in duty or obligation to do. Like many women, when I envisioned my future, I did not anticipate that I would grow older alone. I expected that I would be married with children by the time I was thirty at the latest. Moreover, I felt pressured to be happily coupled.

Simply put, whether or not I would get hitched wasn't even a thought—it was a given. It was a foregone conclusion that I would be settled with a husband and little ones, much like my parents and their parents before them. After all, as a well-educated, well-traveled, and financially secure black woman, why would I not be? Yet as I drifted into my midthirties I found myself and many of my equally successful friends alone.

Let me clarify. We're not alone in the sense that we are isolated or without any connection to anyone. Rather, we are without the one singular connection that is valued by most of society—a significant other. While we all have people that matter in our worlds, such as family and friends, it is the lack of a life partner or a soul mate that stigmatizes us and downplays all of our other accomplishments. No matter what else we have achieved, we are all still bombarded with questions like "Why can't she find a man?" and "Is there something wrong with her?" I must admit that these questions haunted me as my milestone thirtieth birthday approached. Then, on September 11, 2000, something in me shifted when I stumbled across the premiere of a show called *Girlfriends*.

Girlfriends was a half-hour sitcom revolving around the lives of four black women living in California; three of them were single and one of them was married. I was instantly captivated—glued to the set. What drew me in was the image of three positive sisters navigating their way through careers, education, and life without the aid of a man. It was only the second time in my life that I could recall seeing someone like me or my sisters on television in an inspiring way.

Every Monday I'd sit and watch Joan, Lynn, and Toni confront challenges similar to mine and my girlfriends'. It gave me solace knowing that I and my friends weren't the only beautiful and successful women unable to attract a suitable suitor; we weren't alone in the struggle. What I didn't know was how statistics painted an increasingly bleak picture of marriage prospects for black women.

According to the 2005 U.S. Census Bureau data, 70 percent of black women and 61 percent of all women over the age of thirty live alone. This is not surprising considering that over the twenty-year period between 1970 and 2001 the overall marriage rate declined by 17 percent. The drop for black people, 34 percent, was double that for whites. By 2005, data found that 44 percent of black men and 42 percent of black women reported that they had never been married.

I was not aware that the deck was stacked against me as I entered my thirties. I guess, as an avid television watcher, I wouldn't have known, though. With the exception of *Girlfriends*, even in 2000 there were few other shows featuring strong, independent black women making it without a man.

Television had been slightly kinder when reflecting the struggle of single white women. They began to be empowered in the 1970s with the launch of the *Mary Tyler Moore Show*, starring that career-driven woman who moved to a new city for a job at a television station. The show made a point to depict Mary as a woman who was not desperate to find a man. She was happy and fulfilled just living up to her professional potential. When I was young I'd stay up late at night to watch reruns of the show, awed and inspired by Mary Richards. I used to say, "I'm gonna be the black Mary." Still, I yearned for a character that looked and sounded a little more like me.

The Mary Tyler Moore Show wasn't the only one over the years that showed progressive, single white women. In 1976, there was *Alice*, a show with an ensemble cast of single women striving to make their way in the world. Of course, who can forget the eighties, which produced a rash of ensemble shows designed to showcase white women making it against the odds, like *Cagney and Lacey*, *Kate and Allie*, and *Designing Women*. Yet nearly a decade and a half after the white woman revolution began, there were still no independent, single black woman to show me it was OK if I didn't live up to the marriage expectation. Where was the *Julia* for the generation Xers?

I saw my first sassy single black woman on the *Jeffersons*. Florence, played by Marla Gibbs, showed up in 1975. She could give verbal jabs as good as she got; she was confident and bold. Yet she was hard for me to relate to because even at five I knew I aspired to be more than a servant.

A year later *What's Happening* came on, and once again I felt that I was left short. Mabel was a hardworking mother trying to support her two kids. She was no-nonsense, fiercely protective, and determined to carve out a better life for her family. However, she also had a low-paying job and lived in the ghetto—a life I knew nothing about, having been raised in a predominantly white neighborhood with professional parents.

By the time the eighties rolled around I at least got to see upwardly mobile, single, strong black men. There seemed to be a run of them. There was *Benson*, Ricardo Tubbs on *Miami Vice*, Blair Underwood's character on *LA Law*, Denzel Washington's character on *St. Elsewhere*, and Michael Warren's character on *Hill Street Blues*. Sure, there were also more black women on TV, but it appeared to me, even as a child, that there was a clear reason that these sisters were unattached. Nell Carter's character on *Gimme a Break* was overweight and stuck taking care of white kids in a small family home. Anna Maria Horsford's character on *Amen* was desperate and needy. She also still lived at home with her father as a thirty-year-old woman. Jackée's character on *227* also worked a meager job and only got by using her sexuality.

It wasn't until the year I was to graduate from college, 1993, that I had my first glimpse of black female characters that resembled women in my life. *Living Single* focused on four single black women living in Brooklyn; each of them was smart, well employed, educated, and self-reliant. It was in one of those characters, Maxine Shaw, that I saw myself. She was sharp tongued, had a brilliant mind, and felt no need to compromise herself to find a man.

Despite my internal pull to be married and be part of a "we," I found myself wanting to be her and being comfortable with the thought. However, as with all good things, the show came to a screeching halt after just four short years. When *Living Single* was gone, I found myself reverting to conventional needs and wants, including a desire to be Mrs. Somebody. I continued to crave the traditional role of wife and mother and felt inadequate without it until I tuned into *Girlfriends* that random Monday night five years later.

It was *Girlfriends* that guided me back toward the notion that a single, prosperous woman is complete with or without a man on her arm or in her bed. It has again stirred up the beliefs in me that I don't need to sacrifice my talent or blessings to have a husband, that any man who is worth it will accept and respect me as I am. In fact, he will lift me up and make me a better person than I am alone.

While I don't credit *Girlfriends*, *Living Single*, or any other television show with being the only or most powerful factor in my being at peace in my own skin, seeing images of women who embody what I feel innately I am supposed to be fills me with a greater sense of support and gives me the confidence to buck expectation.

I hope other single African American women will realize that although we've been downplayed or ignored in the media, we are not failures simply because we don't have a man. Nor are we disappointments to anyone, unless we fight to rise above the glass ceiling in business yet allow others to define, belittle, or limit the possibilities for our lives based on our lack of a relationship.

As my grandmother told me, there is a huge difference between being alone and being lonely. At some point we all will find ourselves alone; we came into the world alone, and we will leave it that way. Single women can and often do have lives filled with love. The trick is loving yourself even when you are alone and finding people you can love and who will love you back so you will never be lonely.

I Didn't Work This Hard Just To Get Married

Part One

Single in the Spotlight

Eating, sleeping, vacationing, buying a home—all things that many women, no matter their race, never think they'll have to do alone. But, particularly as black women, we should. Statistics show that for every one hundred single black women, there are just seventy single black men. Of course, that doesn't indicate what percentage of these men are in jail. Even supposing that all the men are unattached, the numbers also show that between 1970 and 2001 the percentage of black people that got married dropped by 34 percent. If you're thinking that crossing racial lines will improve your odds of getting married, consider that overall marriage rates have dipped by 17 percent during the same time period. So it would seem that women, especially black women, are steadily finding themselves aging alone.

It would seem to follow that as the number of single people in society rises, the stigma attached to marital status would decrease, but sadly it has not. The percentage of single women now stands at 51 percent according to the census, meaning the majority of women are spouseless. Yet when I and many others run into friends and family, the first questions are generally "Are you married?" or "Who are you dating?" If you answer that you're unattached, you run the risk of being instantly judged. Social psychologist Bella DePaulo explains this phenomenon in her book *Singled Out: How Singles Are Stereotyped, Stigmatized, and Ignored, and Still Live Happily Ever After*. She says other people think that "they understand your emotions: You are miserable and lonely and envious of couples. They know what motivates you: more than anything else in the world, you want to be coupled. If you are a single person of a certain age, they also know why you are not coupled: You are commitment phobic or too picky, or have baggage."[1]

While this assessment may be incorrect, the list of single sistahs seems to be extending into an endless abyss these days, proving U.S. Census data right: the majority of African American women do and will grow old alone. Even celebrities aren't immune to the possibility of a solo existence. Sanaa Lathan, Tracee Ellis Ross, Vivica A. Fox, Elise Neal, Tyra Banks, Naomi Campbell, and even Oprah are absent shiny gold bands. Another notable on that list is the woman consistently named one of the world's most beautiful, Oscar winner Halle Berry. She isn't sporting a diamond these days either, and she says that's by her own design. That may signal a dramatic shift in attitude—it would appear that even Halle Berry has discovered that having a child and a complete, successful life does not require a marriage license.

As more single women in the public eye disprove the expectation that single life is lonely and empty, women in business increasingly find themselves succeeding while still being saddled with the perception that they have floundering personal lives. Although many don't lament their single status, they do often give it thought. So it begs the question: why, no matter what else single women achieve, is their lifestyle viewed with less luster than a diamond solitaire on their third finger? Perhaps the answer is as DePaulo describes:

> The soulmate mythology is the ultimate seduction: Find that one right person and all of your wishes will come true. Find that one perfect person, your All-Purpose Partner, and your path through the rest of your adult life is set. And it will be a happy path, indeed.

We buy into the idea that a mate will be the all-in-one solution to our every need; that if we find one perfect person we'll have a best friend, lover, champion, caregiver, and escort. We'll not only have a mate to help us confront obstacles both big and small, but one with whom we can build a home and wealth, as well as spend vacations.[2]

Still, census data show that women of every race are becoming less and less dependent on a man for financial support and decision making, even though our attitude about needing and wanting a man as a partner has been slow to change. Maybe it's because we believe that marriage is the only cure for loneliness. Perhaps things would shift if we were told that, on average, most of us will spend more years of our lives single than married. Perception would shift, with women more freely admitting that we are alone but not necessarily lonesome.[3]

1

Livin' Single

With Actress and Comedienne Kim Coles

L et's face it: as society struggles to catch up to the growing reality that fewer people yearn to or decide to marry, the idea of finding a mate is still continually pushed. For celebrities, who seemingly have it all, the questions about when they will marry or why they haven't yet are splashed across newspaper and magazine headlines all the time. One wonders if it's more difficult to be single in the spotlight, where women are perceived as having everything going for them—except for living up to the societal expectation of having a husband.

Who better to talk about living single in the public eye than actress and comedienne Kim Coles? In 1993, Coles, Ericka Alexander, Kim Fields, and Dana Owens, aka Queen Latifah, starred in the ground-breaking television show *Living Single*. The show set the groundwork for a discussion of the social life of African American women by following four black women while they tried to navigate the dating and business worlds in New York City. For five years Coles played Synclair James, the naive, dependent, country cousin of a strong self-employed woman. Audiences watched as her innocent and unworldly character met, fell in love with, and married the building's handyman, Overton, who was also the first man who came her way.

In reality, life has been anything but a sitcom for Coles. It has been more like a dramedy—a cross between a comedy and drama. Despite the twists and turns in her personal life, Coles is clear about one thing: she isn't willing to just settle for the first person to come her way. She balks at the fairy tale of a prince coming to sweep a woman off her feet, although she understands why many women buy into that notion. "I think for most of them it's not their fault. . . . It's what society tells them it's supposed to be. I think society has this expectation, and the fairy tales didn't help, not to mention the fact that our mothers and grandmothers all got married. This doesn't help either. I think it has to do with feeling someone chose me. See, I am beautiful, smart, amazing, because someone validated me by saying, 'I'm choosing you and I'm going to walk down the aisle with you.'"

The road to enlightenment hasn't come without its bumps and bruises for Coles, who was married while struggling to establish herself as a comedienne. "I've been married," she says. "I was married when I was twenty-three years old. We were young; we were broke. We didn't even have a wedding, and there is a little piece of me—I'm not going to lie—that says, you know what, before I die, I kind of want a wedding. But I realize it's not because I want a man to choose me, because I've already had that. I kind of want a big party."

Although her marriage didn't last, Coles isn't bitter. Instead she views her divorce as the catalyst for her self-exploration. Coles took time to reevaluate her thoughts about marriage and commitment, something she thinks other women should do. "I think it requires women to think outside the box and go, like, 'Do I really, really want this life, or is it something someone told me I am supposed to have?'"

The answer to that question didn't come easily for Coles. She first had to take a look at her own dating habits before she learned that her main regret wasn't being single but being with the wrong person. "My regret was dating guys I shouldn't, dating guys that were bad for me, so I wouldn't be single," she says. Coles believes the fear of being alone is so ingrained in women that, like her, they are often not consciously aware that they are selecting or staying with someone who doesn't suit them. She says her own awareness only came through a chance encounter.

Coles's epiphany came during a shopping spree a couple of years ago. As the starlet passed a security guard, he innocently asked if she was shopping for clothes for a new boyfriend. That simple sentence stopped her in her tracks. It forced her to take note of how much time she'd spent buying suits from the men's department for various boyfriends. It was so often that she'd lost track—the guard had not.

Coles says, "I dropped out of the dating scene. . . . I was a dating disaster. I realized it was me. I was drawing to myself guys, men, who had either alcohol or drug problems. A guy who was constantly saying, 'I'm in the process of divorcing of my wife,' but he never fully did. Or I'd find out he's crazy. You know, that kind of thing."

So Coles took a long, hard look at herself to figure out why she wasn't attracting the kind of men she wanted in her life, and she says she found that "if you believe *The Secret* or the laws of attraction, if you believe you deserve something better—that there's something better coming, that you're supposed to have something better—then you have a chance. I guess I didn't believe I did, so I stopped dating two years ago. I shut it down."

She went on dating strike, refusing to go out with any man so she could take time to get to know herself. "I said let's work on me first to see what it is about me that's drawing these disastrous relationships." She soon found that her lack of self-esteem made it easy for her to accept whatever person came her way rather than holding fast to her standards and demanding someone who met them. It wasn't until she learned to be happy with who she was as an individual that it became clear to Coles that she was OK on her own, and that if she was going to be with a mate he'd have to add to her life rather than detract from it.

Coles says the kind of man she discovered she was attracted to wasn't drawn to her, in part, because men buy into the societal expectation that a woman with her level of financial security and success is either taken or unattainable. "I think there is an expectation that you are a public person so you must have access to a billion men. . . . For me, the expectation is: 'She probably already has someone so I won't even try to talk to her.' There's an intimidation factor when it comes to me. A man who dates me has to be willing to date my career as well because it's a public career. Someone is going to walk up to the table and interrupt us, and he's got to be OK with that."

While her level of achievement tended to scare off some men, Coles unfortunately found that her means and status were enticing to men who viewed being with her as a step up for them. "It doesn't deter the broke ones. I have no problem attracting the broke ones, because they have nothing to lose." She says the reason that men don't hesitate in approaching a woman, no matter how much greater her means may be than his, is that "one of their common traits is they're often looking for something better. They're always thinking: 'Can I find something better?' I think women settle, and they get happy. They say, 'Well, he's a little pudgy, but I love him.'" She cites as proof that men are motivated to constantly upgrade in their personal life "the famous line 'Show me a man who's dating Halle Berry, and I'll show you a man who's sick of dating Halle Berry.' So I just think that's something men are hardwired, biologically, to do—constantly look for something new and a new place to spread their seed."

Coles says men, conversely, have the expectation that all women, including her, date for the purpose of finding a man to marry and procreate with, but this is definitely a notion with which she cannot identify. "I don't have the same pressures. I don't want children, so I think that knocks away a lot of the needing to be a couple for me." In fact, she says, "If I had one hundred men in front of me, and any of them wanted to have children, I would throw them all [the ones that want kids] back into the dating pool."

While Coles doesn't buy into the idea that marriage and children are the keys to happiness, finding someone with whom to share her life is of interest to her. Coles says she is open to dating any man who has the characteristics she values, and she takes issue with the common expectation that a successful black woman isn't looking to settle down with a man of color. She rejects the notion that women of color with money believe "white is right," even though census data show that black women are exploring options such as interracial dating at greater rates. In 2006, for example, there were 117,000 unions between black women and white men; that number represents a sharp rise over the 95,000 marriages in 2000. Nonetheless, Cole states, "I have to admit, I would really prefer a brother. I would prefer a man of color."

Ultimately, Coles has found that she's happy with who she is, with or without a man. It's a realization she came to only after, she says, "I discovered it is better for me to be single and find a way to be happy than be miserable with some guy just to say I have a boyfriend. To be miserable in a relationship is not better than being single and lonely sometimes. I discovered I enjoy my company. I enjoy other things about myself, so now I won't accept a disastrous relationship. I will see the red flags, and I won't knock them down."

Cole suggests women ask themselves not whether they have a man but whether they have love in their lives. She says, "I don't have a boyfriend, but I have lots of love and that fills me up." Looking at her life in terms of what she does have rather than what she doesn't and being at peace with her present situation are part of developing a better sense of self. Coles says that will serve her best whether she stays single or goes on to find a mate. "I think you have to be a strong single before you can be a strong couple anyway."

Still, if Coles does spend the rest of her life single, she will have no regrets about it. "I don't have any regrets about being single. You know when I have regrets? When I need someone to climb up on a ladder and do something for me. But you know what I do? I call the handyman."

2

Princess Charming

With Author Deborah Gregory

*L*ife *has been anything* but a crystal staircase for author, performer, and writer Deborah Gregory. The creator of the wildly popular Cheetah Girls novel series may be a household name now, but in her childhood she was just another case number in the New York City foster care system.

"I remember my first foster mother. She was an angry woman, and she had a very derogatory opinion of men. She was from the South and quite a drinker. She would say, 'Yeah, when you got one coming in the door, you just get the other one moving out the back.' I remember seeing this. She was married, and not an attractive woman, especially when the glasses came off and the teeth came out. I look back now and marvel that she got some man to marry her who was never there, and she got other men. She was slipping on the side."

Gregory's story of neglect is unfortunate, but even worse, it isn't unique. According to the Adoption and Foster Care Analysis Reporting System, 32 percent of all children in foster care are African American. Disproportionately, these same kids will remain in the system until age eighteen without being adopted or getting a permanent home. Life afterward doesn't look bright for them either: 84 percent of the kids studied in the report became parents before the age of twenty-one, 51 percent were unemployed, and 25 percent had been homeless, while yet another 30 percent were receiving public assistance. Only 54 percent of them got their high school diplomas, and just 2 percent of foster children earned a college degree.

Gregory beat the odds, obtaining both an associate's degree and a bachelor's degree. She has also supported herself quite well using the talent for reading and writing she developed as a little girl. "I grew up so lonely. I was an avid reader. When I went to bookstores, the characters in the books were so white. It was very hurtful, so I wanted to create something for girls of all colors that would make them feel pretty." Remarkably, for a generation of preteen and teenage girls, that's exactly what she's done with the Cheetah Girls.

If you aren't up on pop culture and don't have a teenage girl in your life, you may not know who the Cheetah Girls are. Their names are Galleria, Chanel, Aquanetta, and Dorinda. Their ethnicity is unclear, and, like Gregory, one of them is a foster child. The quartet leaped from the pages of Gregory's novels to the small screen in a 2003 Disney Channel movie. The flick starring Raven-Symoné, Adrienne Bailon, Kiely Williams, and Sabrina Bryan was produced by diva Whitney Houston. Its success led to another movie and a hit soundtrack, which both shared the same message: young girls should rely on their instincts, intellect, and decision-making powers to fulfill their dreams despite obstacles and adversity.

"If you notice the drive of the characters in Cheetah Girls and *Catwalk*," Gregory says, the latter the title of her latest novel about the fashion industry, "the main focus is to manifest their dreams. How are they going to do it—navigate things and deal with problems with their family and friends? In a way, it kind of says all that other stuff is nonsense so we don't deal with it."

The nonsense Gregory refers to is focusing on men and relationships rather than aspirations. Although she didn't achieve her early goal of being a singer, Gregory didn't let a longing for a partner stop her from being self-sufficient and becoming a successful novelist. Gregory learned early in life that no one was going to save her from foster care. "I wasn't raised to be married. I was raised in foster homes. I was raised with very low expectations, unfortunately." To combat them, she decided to elevate herself from loneliness and poverty on her own.

"We should stop teaching our children these things, teaching our girls these things, the Cinderella fantasy. My girlfriend, an actress, says she still has this Cinderella thing, this thing in the back of her mind that someone will save her." Gregory made a conscious effort to make sure her multiethnic characters in the Cheetah Girls did not embrace the fantasy. "None of them has the fantasy that some guy is going to come along."

Her unshakable resolve to not rely on men or marriage to fill the void left from her youth only partially explains why she is happily single. To hear her tell it, Gregory has had a steady stream of suitors, yet she never found the need to settle down. "I do not think for a second I feel incomplete without a man. I think if you don't have friends or a close family, you could be lonely, but I'm not. I have a lot of regrets in my life, but not being married or having children is certainly not among them."

Determined and headstrong, she's also decided that not wanting to get married doesn't mean she can't have male companionship at all. "We need them [men] for companionship, but not if they are broke down." Gregory believes that until she finds a suitable mate or needs assistance, she'll go it alone. "I do see myself when I am old with someone, 'cause that's when you need them. Over seventy, I think it would be nice to have a companion to live with, but before then I can have boyfriends. I don't have to live with a man, and I certainly don't have to be married."

Gregory knows that by being unwilling to be flexible about her standards she may have to wait a long while for the right man, so she's come up with a backup plan. "I was in an arts-and-crafts store, and I saw a hand-painted leopard cane that an artist had painted, and I said, 'Let me buy that.' So I now have a cane I can use for support when I am older."

She wishes more women would refuse to lower their expectations about a partner so they could stop being short-changed in relationships. "The truth is that most black women have settled. I see a lot of settling going on on women's parts, putting up with things that they wouldn't if there was more of a pool to draw from."

Gregory says what she's seen on the singles scene has made her often-times think that being by herself is better than simply choosing from the men available. "The biggest problem I find with men—and I meet a lot of men—is that most of them are emotionally damaged; they have a lot of emotional problems. They don't achieve. They don't succeed. They have a lot of baggage." Still, like a lot of black women, she's not willing to give up on African American men and consistently date outside of her race. "The majority of black women tend to like black men; that's definitely put a damper on my choices. Nine times out of ten, they [black men] aren't as emotionally balanced as I am. I've done a lot of work on myself. I don't see them working on themselves."

Gregory believes that if more black women recognized that making a bad choice is to their own detriment, they might also choose to face life solo. "There is nothing worse than a bad relationship. It can kill you, literally."

Constantly working on improving her self-worth and being willing to walk away from the wrong relationships have allowed Gregory to find her inner Cheetah Girl: "grown power" to be a woman who is fierce, tough, and still vulnerable—all qualities she hopes to inspire in the next generation of ethnic women through her writings so they can be their own "Princesses Charming."

3

SSIC: Single Sistah in Charge

With Executive Susan Chapman

Female celebrities certainly aren't the only women who find themselves up for public scrutiny because of their relationship status. Top-notch businesswomen who've spent years carving out niches for themselves in the traditionally male-dominated workforce also find themselves facing judgmental questions about marriage despite the enormous contribution that they make to businesses' bottom lines. It makes one wonder when or if the professional contributions of women will ever outweigh the perceived necessity for them to have a husband or partner in their life to be considered successful.

Women Employed, an organization founded in 1973 to advocate for women's economic advancement, says that as of 2004, 68 million women were in the civilian workforce in United States; that's about 47 percent of all workers. Its numbers show that 65 percent of all African American women work, a percentage greater than that for women of all other races and ethnicities.

These black women are ensuring their financial health by opening their own businesses at an increasing rate. A 2006 study by economist Ying Lowrey in the Small Business Administration's Office of Economic

Research found that black women owned 547,341 companies in 2002, up 75 percent from five years before. And that trend has continued.

The facts seem to support the theory that financial freedom — women's in particular — is high on the list of social changes that have empowered many single people. Women are no longer tethered to husbands for economic life support.[1]

Conversely, the picture for black men is quite bleak, creating difficulties for black women interested in finding a mate of the same race. According to a Henry J. Kaiser Family Foundation study in 2006, there were 4.5 million African American men between the ages of fifteen and twenty-nine in this country, which accounts for 14 percent of all men in this age category. Yet fewer than 8 percent of them had graduated from college, while 17 percent of white men and 35 percent of Asian men earned a degree. This may partially explain why young black men were twice as likely to be unemployed as white or Asian men in 2005.

Even more disappointing is the rate of incarceration. Of African American men ages eighteen to twenty-nine, 10 percent were in prison in 2005 — about 40 percent of the total prison population. Black men between fifteen and twenty-nine were also one and a half times more likely to die at a young age than white or Asian men in 2003. The leading causes of their early demises are suicide, homicide, and unintentional injury. Not far behind is HIV; it was the sixth-leading cause of death according to a July 2006 fact sheet from the Henry J. Kaiser Foundation.

A year later, when Michael Ross wrote his 2006 *Newsweek* article entitled "Report Offers Grim Forecast for Young Black Men," it was clear things for black men hadn't improved much. In it, he states that, according to the U.S. Census, 16 percent of black men in their twenties were behind bars. For African American men who dropped out of high school, the picture was even more bleak. According to Ross, by the time these men reach their early thirties, 60 percent of them will have spent time in prison. And, as if that's not bad enough, African Americans are seven times more likely to go to jail than whites. The correlation between education and prosperity in this society is undeniable; it's a connection that's supported by the fact that "in 2000, about 65 percent of black male high school dropouts had no jobs, either because they couldn't find work or because they were in jail. By 2004, the studies found that number had grown to 72 percent."[2]

Despite the dismal progress of black men in society, women like executive Susan Chapman haven't given up on them as prospects for a lifelong partnership. "I would say that when you reach a certain level of career success as an African American woman, it certainly makes a difference, especially if your desire is to date African American men, because in large measure they are often socialized to feel they are supposed to be the provider and to take care of you, and that's usually financial. So if you make a significant amount more money than they do, then that's a challenge for them." She continues by saying that her main requirement for a man is that he's confident. "It takes a very strong man, whether he's black, green, brown, purple, or blue, to have a woman who's achieved a level of career success more than he has and be OK with that."

Without a prospective husband on the horizon, she's not putting her goals on hold. She's forged ahead with home ownership, financial stability, and now motherhood, all of which she knows are intimidating to a lot of men. She's aware that a man often feels as if his main role in a committed relationship is to be the breadwinner so that he can lead his family—making all of the decisions on how money is spent or where they live. But, she says, unlike a lot of women, "I'm not beholden to anyone for financial support or for that kind of provision, which may be threatening to men." However, Chapman says that her self-confidence, which has been stoked by her family and faith, make it impossible for her to undercut her own goals and achievements merely to boost a man's ego. She firmly believes that her potential partner will respect her independence rather than fear it.

But having a seat in the boardroom at Citigroup Realty Services doesn't keep Chapman from being stigmatized for choosing to take on so many roles solo. Her professional acumen seems to fall away when people notice the absence of a ring on her finger. However, she's learned to shrug off the assessments of others. "I learned about ten years or so ago about setting my own measure of success. So I don't look to others for validation."

Chapman may not seek it, but she's certainly drawn a lot of admiration for her business sense. As the head of global operations she oversees more than fourteen thousand properties in nearly ten countries; it's a position that she knows puts her light-years ahead of potential suitors. It's a reality she has accepted. Moreover, it's a truth that does not bother her because she believes that if she eventually finds a husband, he will be a man who will embrace her achievements. "My whole thing is I don't want to just check the box to say 'I'm married.' I want to be married to someone who is my partner, who wants to work with me, who shares the same values that I do, who thinks it's OK that my face shows up in *Essence* or *Black Enterprise* and gets excited about that. My thing is if that's not what I'm going to have, then I don't want it."

Knowing what she wants and how to get it has earned Chapman a place in the inner sanctum of corporate America, where she is one of few blacks or women. And while she is responsible for some three hundred thousand employees, she is able to balance her private and professional lives, in spite of what others think. "There is a misperception that when you have a very high-powered career, if you want to call it that, all you do is work and all you do is travel. You know, my life is no different than anybody else's. I don't see the stresses of my job being any different than my mom's were as a nurse, and she had four kids."

Chapman doesn't yet have children of her own, but she takes time to mentor young girls, an endeavor she believes is essential to building their self-esteem. Her own journey to self-assuredness took time. "I think earlier in my life, when I didn't have this level of career success and financial stability, I felt the need and desire to change who I was, to try to tone it down so guys felt more comfortable to date me. But I've learned I am who I am." She's no longer willing to inflate a man's ego by downplaying her own accomplishments.

Chapman is a graduate of Vanderbilt University, the University of Massachusetts at Amherst, and the University of Wisconsin. According to *Black Enterprise Magazine,* she was dubbed one of the "Most Powerful [African American] Players" in business. She now looks at all her achievements with unabashed pride. "My approach to it [my career] has been that God put me on this Earth for a reason. There is a certain level of gifts and talents he's given me. Shame on me if I try to hide them."

Her spirituality is something that guides her in every avenue of her life, including her dating life. "I believe that God put you here for a reason, and that if you are bold enough to trust him with every aspect of your life *except* your relationship, that's not really faith." It's her faith, financial means, and sense of self that allow her to walk away without apology from relationships that don't fill her needs. "We [successful women] have choices. If something is not working for Susan, I choose something else."

In addition to crediting God for her business prowess, she gives praise to her parents. "My parents have never been the kind of people to say you're nothing without a man. They've been exactly the opposite in terms of encouraging me to grow and develop in my career." However, it was her mother that was her beacon to the top. Chapman says her mother was the one who told her she could achieve anything she put her mind to, and her mother led by example. "My mom, I look at her as one of the breakouts. She always made more money than my dad, and my father had a problem with it, but my mother was like, 'Whatever—I'm just going to do what I am supposed to be doing.' And she ended up having a fabulous career as an oncology nurse."

Chapman expects that she will lean on her family if she chooses to go through with her plan to adopt a child as a single woman. "You depend on your family to be supportive. I don't think that you can realistically raise a child by yourself. Nobody can, whether you are working or not. You're going to need help at some point, so it's just a matter of putting the right things in place so you can have the support that you need."

Making the decision to become a mother alone wasn't difficult for Chapman at all. "It's been more important to me to be a parent before this is all over, but clearly you don't have to be married to do that. I would love to be married to do that, but if it doesn't happen, I am certainly still planning on having kids." She is already putting the pieces in place so that her child will have the same level of love and support that she had as a child. "Family and close friends are very important to me, so I want my kids to have a relationship with their aunts and uncles and my friends and my parents."

Chapman isn't alone in the quest to become a mother by adoption without a spouse. The number of single black women choosing to pursue motherhood alone has been on a steady upswing. According to the U.S. Department of Health and Human Services' Children's Bureau, more than half of the fifty thousand kids placed in permanent homes in the United States were adopted by African American women without a spouse.[3]

There's almost no doubt Chapman will follow through on her plan to start a family on her own. She's a woman who has certainly reached many of her other goals.

"When I purchased my first home, to me it was just another goal I set for myself. Maybe because I've always had a realistic view of how things are. The realistic situation is I would love to be married and in a fantastic relationship, but I know a lot of people who are married and miserable." If she does don a wedding ring, Chapman has made it clear that the person will be the right fit for her. "I don't want something that's not good for me. I see a lot of people settling, and that's never been how I am." Otherwise, she'll happily go it alone. "If I'm going to get married, I only want to do it once and keep it moving."

As Chapman moves toward her goal of sharing her life and love with a child, she says if there is a man that goes along with the package, she'd be thrilled. But "if I don't ever become a mom, I'll be disappointed. If I don't ever become a wife, I'll get over it."

Part Two

Mother May I: Single Mothers Ruling the Roost

As children many of us played the game Mother May I, oblivious that this game reflected reality for many children who have only one parent, usually a mother, to ask for permission to participate in daily activities. The 2007 census says the number of single-parent households has remained at about 9 percent from 1994 to 2006; that's up from 5 percent in 1970. In raw numbers, there were about 12.9 million one-parent families in the United States in 2006; 10.4 million of them were homes headed by an unmarried mother.

It's a reality that hasn't been overlooked in African American movies since the 1974 Oscar-nominated film *Claudine*, starring Diahann Carroll. In it, Carroll plays a struggling mother of six trying to manage her brood while finding time to have a relationship with a character played by James Earl Jones. What's striking about this film isn't just that it was ahead of the upswing in women acting as heads of their household. The film also captures two issues single mothers today still wrestle with: how and if they should find time to date, and how they can lift their family out of poverty.

You see, statistics show that life for families without two parents is often full of money woes—even as black women earn more degrees than their male counterparts. Partly it can be explained by the fact that women earn less than men for the same or comparable jobs. The AFL-CIO found in 2007 that female workers make seventy-seven cents for every dollar earned by a man. However, when race is added to that equation, African American women fared even worse, taking home only sixty-eight cents for every dollar paid to a man.

For women who are single following a divorce, the dramatic shift in family income can be terrifying, prompting some to try to find a new partner immediately to restore the financial balance. But the 2002 National Survey of Family Growth from the Department of Health and Human Services found that while 54 percent of all divorced women remarry in five years, only 32 percent of black women enter a second marriage during that time, which means African American women are more likely to have to figure out how to be self-sufficient.

A preponderance of black single mothers is figuring out how to navigate life and financial responsibilities alone; some of them are even doing so happily. Why? Because for many of them, the idea of going through the heartbreak again, exposing their children to new men, and giving up their new-found independence is not something they relish. Rather, these women believe that being a powerful force of one can be as good as, if not better than, being part of a dysfunctional twosome.

4

The Enjoli Woman Is Dead

With Single Mother Jackie DeVaughn

"*We still hold on* to the idea that you're supposed to be the worker and homemaker. I call it the 'Enjoli Woman' syndrome—that we're supposed to bring home the bacon and fry it up in the pan. Honestly I can't stand that woman now because realistically I can't do all the things that heifer did then. The pressures on me are too great; greater than they were on women back then. Back then, my mom could be more of a domestic than I can now. Unfortunately, our culture still wants to perpetuate that idea. I think it caters to the male ego. You can't ask a woman to cook, make six figures, and raise your children so you can watch the game; that ain't going to happen," says Jackie DeVaughn, a divorced mother of two.

Enjoli was a popular perfume that came out in the late 1970s. The commercial, which seemed to be constantly playing on TV, featured a jingle sung by a woman who claimed, "I can bring home the bacon, fry it up in the pan, and never let you forget you're a man, 'cause I'm a woman—Enjoli."[1] The perfume may be discontinued now, but the idea of a woman who succeeds in the boardroom while being subservient at home stuck, much to the dismay of generations of women who have tried to live up to that impossible pledge.

DeVaughn tried to do it all during her marriage, which eventually ended after fifteen years. In that time, she tried to be everything to everybody except herself. "I lost myself in a marriage, and I am finding myself now outside of that. I know who I am more so now than I did then."

Then, she was a woman struggling to keep a picture-perfect family together at the cost of her own career. "For me, I was financially sound before we [my husband and I] moved with our kids to Texas for a new beginning. Prior to that, I had a career with the city of Los Angeles. So when I got there [Texas] I didn't have a job, but moving back to L.A. after the divorce, I was able to jump back in and was a bit better off financially."

DeVaughn was lucky. She was able to get an analyst job in Los Angeles and get back on her feet. However, a study by two University of California economists found that divorce affects black children far more than white children. Statistics show that in the first two years after a divorce, the income of a black family declines by more than half, while white family earnings goes down by about 30 percent. African American families very rarely make up the lost income, while white households usually rebound, recouping about a third of the funds absent after a divorce. The sad fact is that poverty is a reality for many black families once the parents split.[2]

One reason that black women don't fare as well as their white counterparts following divorce is that African American mothers are often already working and earning at the same income level before a relationship split, something white women have not done while married. Certainly, that is the case for DeVaughn, who worked consistently throughout her marriage. It wasn't until she and her husband filed for divorce and set up two separate households that she began to worry about whether she'd be able to make ends meet while taking care of her daughters on her own. "As we were going through the process of the divorce, he took advantage of trying to dump stuff on me. So it lent itself to some financial difficulty at times, but it was a matter of me making adjustments."

DeVaughn didn't let the brief financial strain she came under change her attitude about men though. "I think there are some [women] that may have bitterness, but I don't. I don't have an aversion to men. Coming out of my marriage, my marriage wasn't—or should I say didn't start—on the right foundation to sustain itself." She says it took a lot of evaluation for her to be at peace with the demise of her marriage. "I recognize what I did wrong. I compromised my principles in my first marriage, and I do see there are other possibilities out there for me."

She says she eased back into dating, making it clear that finding a man isn't her priority. "I kind of closed myself off to men even making advances when I was first going through the process of divorce. When I did open myself up, I got more hits as a single mother than my girl-friends who are just single." She thinks that might be because perpetu-ally single women are not open to men who don't immediately fit their criteria. "I think there are some women who may have been single for a long period of time, and their scope completely narrows and they're not as flexible as someone who has been in a relationship before." It's her battle scars from her previous marriage that make DeVaughn careful not to relinquish her self-reliance to potential suitors. She keeps them away from her children so they know she is capable of taking care of herself and her family on her own.

Having been in a relationship doesn't stop others from pressuring DeVaughn to jump back into a new one. Having a partner or believing that every woman should have a mate is something DeVaughn thinks is ingrained in our society. "I think culturally we are still defined by who we are with and whether or not we have a family unit [a husband and kids], even though the whole marriage thing has been played out." But she says one surefire way to stop the nagging and the questions about finding a new partner is being happy with who you are. "If we exhibit the happiness of what we do, it can lend itself to not even having the discussion of your relationship status come up. Oftentimes when people find you are so full of life in all the avenues you partake in, there won't be a need to ask 'Do you need or have a man?'"

While DeVaughn says she does enjoy the company of a man from time to time, she is relishing her time alone. Getting married again is something she isn't rushing into. "Everyone loves companionship, I believe, but coming through [hardship] and being single are times to identify who you really are. I think sometimes, as women, we sacrifice ourselves for different relationships, whether it's with our spouses or our children. But it's time alone that gives us an opportunity for self-definition."

She says being by herself also gives her time to be an example to her daughters, showing them that there's nothing wrong with being single. "I know that my kids look at me as a role model, so some of the things that I've gone through I wouldn't want them to think they have to." She knew that it was important for her to be OK so that they could be emotionally sound.

DeVaughn admits that being a role model as a single mother isn't easy, but the key to making it work is seeking help from family and friends. "I believe it takes a village to raise a child. I would love the male perspective for my girls, but I think I'm OK because they have their cousins. They still have their dad. We've created our own village with our friend subsets. You just have to take a different option to fill the voids." One gap she's not trying to fill is the one of father. "As far as I am concerned, they have a dad, and I would never replace him. I try to make sure they understand that."

She also tries to make sure they have a healthy attitude about men and relationships. Part of that is keeping her dating life private and separate from her life with them. "The men that I did or have been dating, one in particular, his response was: 'That's great because I have kids of my own.' Another guy that I dated doesn't have kids at all, and he's cool. He's trying to take an interest in my children's activities." DeVaughn says that despite conventional wisdom, the men she's met have no aversion to a woman with kids. "There are more guys that are happy to find women who are not looking for children or to have them—at least in my age group."

If a man didn't want her because of her children, DeVaughn couldn't care less. She says she'll be just fine if she doesn't get married again. "After you come out of a relationship, you do a self-evaluation. You prioritize certain things, and you may not put the effort into dating." While she's willing to try her hand at dating, her expectations about what she wants from a relationship and from men have changed. She's now willing to give only a piece of herself to a relationship unless she finds a suitable mate. "I will put forth the effort into a relationship, but that person must exhibit traits that make me want to put the effort out there. I am going to hold back to a certain point." However, if a man who respects her relationship with her children, her self-sufficiency, and her career drive comes along, she would be willing to lower some of the emotional walls she's put up.

DeVaughn says she's cautious in relationships because she wants to set an example for her girls, to show them they can have a happy, fulfilling life without a man in it. And, should they choose to have a mate in their life, that they know he must be worth the hard work and sacrifice. She says educating them about finding personal fulfillment and forming healthy relationships is her most important goal at this point in her life. If nothing else, she wants to make sure they know that while they can't be all things to all people, they can be the best woman they can—just not the Enjoli woman.

5

I Can Do Bad by Myself

With Single Mother and Student Pamela Harris

"*It's absolutely better* to be single than be with the wrong person," says Pamela Harris, a divorced mother with two young boys who walked away from her marriage when she came to the realization that the relationship wasn't meeting her needs. "I cried a lot of nights, but I didn't want my kids to grow up in that environment."

It was her fervor for a better life for her children that gave Harris the strength to move forward without her husband and without a constant male presence for her kids. She says all women who feel trapped in a miserable relationship should consider improving their situations, if not for themselves, then for their kids. "You can put your mind to do something. Don't let a man determine who you are. You determine who you are and who you're going to be."

Harris decided she would rather be a single parent than be in an unhappy marriage. Yet, even though her union was not ideal, leaving was still heart wrenching. "At one point I thought, 'I can't do this,' but I felt like I had to do what I had to do." It was an effort well spent and a challenge that she says women should know is surmountable. "So many times I feel that women, even those with one child, feel like 'How can I do it? I can't make it.' I look at them and say, 'It's not that bad. You can survive. You can do this.'"

Harris's courage in knowing that she could do it on her own came from her upbringing. "It's been instilled in me since I was a kid that you don't need a man to do it all." Harris watched her mother raise two kids alone after her divorce. "My mom and dad divorced when I was two, so I was raised by just my mom and my sister. My mom made us do things." She says she was taught to do basic home repairs and pay bills. She learned by example how to maintain a household while managing a career. Although there was no man in her home, she absorbed skills from the other men in her family. "My uncles and cousins taught us how to paint and how to fix stuff. My mom and I still go to Home Depot and take the classes."

She says knowing how to take care of herself and owning her home have boosted her self-esteem. "Men think that dating a woman with children means that she just needs someone to take care of her and her kids. I make it clear: I can take care of these kids and myself." Harris wears her independence like a badge of honor, a testament to the fine job her single mother did. "It comes from how we—my sister and I—were raised."

Harris admits that being the mother of two young boys is her personal joy, but it's been a hindrance as she dips back into the dating pool. "The men that I've talked to about my boys say they don't date women with boys because they believe that when boys get to a certain point, they feel they are the men of the house, so as your male partner they won't get the respect they deserve from the children." She says that the men she's been out with tell her there's a clock running on her to find a mate who will accept her kids. "Even gentlemen I've been out with have said, 'You'd better hurry up and get married because once they get to a certain age, you're going to be off the market.'"

But Harris says she's not concerned about pairing up with someone just to satisfy the male ego. "Men tend to be babies themselves—it's just that they don't want to share the spotlight." She says she's resolved herself to being single for quite some time so she can focus on giving her boys all of the guidance they need. "Looking at the men today, I think my boys may have a better shot at being taught how to be a man from me than by a man who is not, in my opinion, a real man."

Still, Harris says she yearns for companionship but wants to protect her kids, refusing to expose them to a string of random men. "Dating is really difficult, especially because I don't want that around my children." So she makes sure not to bring anyone home early in a relationship. "Until I want that person around them, I can't have that interaction with my kids."

Harris thinks her children aren't the only reason it is challenging to find a man. She says her success level is also a major intimidation to men. "As I move up as an executive, it is very difficult. A friend of mine told me that I need to find my husband now, 'cause once I get my Ph.D. it's going to become a big issue." But Harris won't buy into the idea that she should settle for someone who would be intimidated by her success. She's clear about wanting a man who is on the same professional and financial level as herself. "A man is going to have to be able to meet me financially." Aware of the statistics about black men, she knows that may mean she has to date someone of another race or ethnicity. "The time may have come that I have to make the decision to date outside my race."

Regardless of the color or background of a potential partner, Harris is also equally adamant that maturity level is a major component in any relationship she may have. "I have two kids, so I am not going to raise someone else's son. It's not my business to raise a grown man. He has to bring what's needed to the table." Harris is stern about her wants and needs because she was lax about them during her first marriage. But she believes that her divorce taught her enough about herself that she will do better if she gets a second chance at love. "I think you learn a lot that first time you are married. By that second marriage, you know what's expected—you know what you're supposed to do." The difference is, she thinks, that first timers go in expecting the "happily ever after," which may never come. "You have this fairy tale going in, then reality sets in. You weren't prepared to put in that kind of work."

She says she's willing to do the work should a man who fits her criteria cross her path. "There is a list, I have a list. But I will only look at it when a man can fit everything on that list. Then he's the right man for me." She's unapologetic about the fact that she knows what she wants and won't settle for less from a mate. "I have to be. I won't accept anything less. I won't compromise." Given her high standards, she knows that it's possible that most suitors fall short, a reality she accepts wholeheartedly. "If I do find someone else that's fine. If I don't, that's fine as well."

If there is no "Mr." for her, Harris is prepared to continue acting as both Mom and Dad. "I buy myself a gift for Father's Day and one for Mother's Day." For Harris, assuming dual roles as mother and father may be challenging, but it came effortlessly. "It was an easy adjustment because my husband did nothing; nothing much changed for me."

This demanding schedule leaves her very little time for herself. But she's willing to sacrifice a lot of personal time to make sure she's there for her kids. "We do vacations together, then when the kids are out of school, my mom will take them and I will go out of town."

For her children the transition to a single-parent home hasn't been without confusion and a yearning to have a two-parent household. "My kids ask me, 'Are you going to ever get married? Are we going to ever have a dad?' And I think, 'Wow, that's a problem for me.'" While Harris would love to fill her children's craving for a male role model, she knows that if he has to come in the form of a husband for her, it will require her to open herself up in a way she isn't ready for right now. "I'm set in my ways, so I know being with someone will be a difficult adjustment for me." She's willing to make changes to include someone new, always keeping in mind that "a person cannot define you."

But Harris is not willing to lose herself or the gains she's made since her divorce just for the sake of having another man in her life. She's not lonely because she likes who she is and the direction of her life. If that leads her to a new man, then she is ready for it. She says, "I don't have to have someone. It would be nice, but I don't have to have that." Without a man, it's certain that she will just continue to do the best by her children on her own.

6

Baby Mama, No Drama

With Mother and "Father" Lisa Parker

"*How can you grow apart* when your relationship has lasted longer than most marriages?" It's a question that Lisa Parker asked herself when her relationship with her college sweetheart fell apart after the better part of a decade together. They may not have exchanged rings, but during the eight-year span of their relationship she and her partner had seen each other through numerous life-altering events—none more important than the birth of their son. So it's understandable that she mourns the loss of her boyfriend just as deeply as any woman who divorces her husband.

"I'm a single black woman," begins Parker as she describes how her first love blossomed into a long-term affair. "I graduated in 1997 with a degree in economics from Penn State University. At that time I was in a relationship for three, maybe four, years. We continued that relationship, but it became long distance because he moved to California."

In many instances an out-of-town romance falls apart soon after the couple separates geographically, but that wasn't the case for Parker and her man. The pair continued seeing each other as often as possible while building individual lives. "After I graduated from school, I got a job with the Vanguard Group [in Philadelphia]. Nothing fancy, just entry level, but I figured it was a foot in the door to a financial institution that could take me far in life." Her position did develop into something more lucrative, but it didn't take her across country to be with her boyfriend.

Despite that, they continued to get together whenever either was in town, which led to an unanticipated result. "We expected a child and I was like, 'Oh, wow.' It was a shock to my system because I didn't want to be a parent. It would have been nice to be married but that wasn't something I wanted in my life at that time either."

Parker says she remembers a time when she and the father of her child discussed getting married, but she wasn't ready to commit to it nor did she realize he was serious about his intent to make her his wife. She says it may be that this casual conversation before their child was born helped her ex form the idea that she didn't want to be with him. She says he asked what her thoughts were about marriage, to which she replied, "'Marriage is superficial. Why do I have to be married to be with you?' I remember at the time he was really hurt about it."

Still, she says there were no blatant signs that her lack of interest in marriage put an irreparable strain on their relationship. However, it wasn't long before the joyous time in her life was overshadowed by the growing emotional distance between the pair. "It was January 1999, that's when communication started breaking down. A lot of stuff happened, mainly because he was still in California. In September, we had a little boy." Even though her ex remained in another state after the birth, she still felt they were very much coparents—that is, until she realized that a couple of years had gone by. "Our son was two years old, and he [the father] was still playing basketball in California." While he continued to follow his dream to be a professional player, she decided she needed to start making plans for a future for just her and her son. "In my head, I knew we should be together and raising this child." But she then thought, "I can't wait my life out for a person who doesn't know what he wants to do."

Parker didn't wait. She moved in with her sister and began saving money to accomplish her goals. At the top of the list was setting up a permanent place that she and her young son could call home. "Two weeks before my thirtieth birthday, I purchased my house. There was a lifting, like, 'Whew, I finally got something on my own besides my son.'"

Then came another major decision: figuring out what role her absentee boyfriend would play in her and her son's lives. "It's great to be independent . . . but that gets really old, especially when you have a child. I relied on him [my ex] to give him [my son] input, but he wasn't giving it." That concerned Parker because the one thing she promised herself as a child was that should she ever have children they would have a father in their lives, a relationship she lacked in her own childhood.

She's not alone. Parker's circumstance is one in which many black women find themselves. An article in the *Washington Post* found that girls being raised without a father often have problems in relationships.[1] Parker says, "I am a very independent person who didn't have a father figure in my life. My mother was a single parent. Her mother, my grandmother, was a single parent. There were strong black women in our family, so there was no question I could do it alone. You don't need a man to do a lot of things; you can do them yourself."

She states, "After a lot of soul searching and talking to men I knew, I wanted to figure out how to take on the role of my son's dad." But try as she might, Parker quickly realized that while she could be the best mother to her son, giving him all the love and financial support possible, she still lacked the personal knowledge of growing up as a black man in society that she could pass along to her child. "We [women] can raise a perfectly eloquent-speaking black man, but when I walk the street, men don't talk to me the way they talk to each other."

Parker is on to something. An observation that came out of a gathering of Pentecostal clergy and the Seymour Institute for Advanced

Christian Studies is that black boys grow up to become problematic men if they lack a father figure in their home: "Father absence is the bane of the black community, predisposing its children (boys, especially, but increasingly girls as well) to school failure, criminal behavior, and economic hardship, and to an intergenerational repetition of the grim cycle."[2] However, these negative patterns and traits can be reversed or avoided if a young boy is exposed to positive male role models.

Recognizing that she didn't want her son to exhibit anti-social behavior, Parker once again turned to her son's father for guidance, and this time he was there; choosing to move from the West Coast back to Philadelphia so he could be closer to his child. She's now been in her house for three years, and a lot has changed. "In the past three years, his dad came home; that was about a year ago, but we are not together." She says by returning to the area, her ex gets to spend more time with their son. She adds that he is an excellent father, picking their son up often so he can spend time with him and providing him with a positive role model.

Parker's situation isn't a rarity. But she and her ex have been able to put their past relationship differences aside to raise their child. Those who face ongoing strife as unmarried parents are burdened with the label "baby mama drama."

UrbanDictionary.com says a "baby mama" is "the mother of your illegitimate and usually accidental baby." And baby mamas have become the norm in the black community. According to U.S. Census data from 2004, about 60 percent of black women who gave birth were unmarried. This is a stark about-face for African American families, which, despite slavery, at one time regularly forged and maintained two-parent households. According to research, "In 1890, 80 percent of African American families were headed by two parents."[3] Today, however, the number of children born to married black women has taken a sharp nose-dive. So much so that some claim that without "out-of-wedlock childbearing, the African American population would not only fail to reproduce itself, but would rapidly die off."[4] For black children brought into the world by an unmarried mother, the odds of ever having a father present are almost nonexistent, especially considering the fact that the 2005 census showed that 70 percent of African American women were single.

So, why is single parenthood perpetuated in the black community? The answer is unclear. It's still debatable how to stem it or how it has reached epidemic proportions. Some, like columnist William Raspberry, theorize that it may be "that black America's almost reflexive search for outside explanations for our internal problems delayed the introspective examination that may have slowed the trend. . . . For the first time since slavery, it is no longer possible to say with assurance that things are getting better."[5] While the number of births within marriages are not improving, acceptance of children born out of wedlock and women's comfort level with being single parents has increased.

The black church is often cited as aiding this attitude change. During the civil rights era, religious institutions shaped the values of the black community, often inspiring men and women to stick together in order to overcome oppression. Following that period, as economic and social opportunities opened up for African Americans, the family unit began to disintegrate, and the black church did little to reverse the trend. U.S. Census reports show that between 1980 and 2000, the percentage of African Americans over the age of fifteen that have never married nearly doubled to about 45 percent, foreshadowing the current state of black marriage.

Concurrently, church attendance and spirituality among African Americans remained high, even while the values of chastity and marriage were waning in the community. Instead of vehemently speaking out or urging congregants to embrace morality and condemn behavior that was detrimental to the black family, African American churches mainly remained silent; a failure to react to the growing crisis, which was criticized at a 2005 gathering of religious leaders:

Interestingly, they [a gathering of Pentecostal clergy and the Seymour Institute for Advanced Christian Studies] blamed the black church for abetting the decline of the black family—by moderating, virtually out of existence, its once stern sanctions against extramarital sex and childbirth and by accepting present trends as more or less inevitable.[6]

Parker admits that she was not concerned at all about what religion says or what other people would think of her choice to be a single mother. In fact, for her, choosing to raise her son on her own had more to do with her difficulty in letting go of her independence. "My issue with being single is understanding what a man really has to offer an independent woman." Because she's taken on the responsibility for not only her son but herself, being vulnerable to a man and allowing him to care for her is something she constantly has to talk herself into. "I don't know how to bring myself down to the point that I need someone else."

And while she is proud of her role as mother to her own child, Parker is opposed to dating a man who is a single father and says, "I don't really want a man that has a child." Her past experiences with a couple of men with children have soured her on the possibility. She says in the first instance, the man made it clear that his time with his children was theirs alone, leaving her out of the equation all together. "Another guy I dated who had his son every other weekend said, 'I don't really introduce women to my son.'" She says she was stunned because she'd been in a long-term relationship with this man and thought they were building toward a lasting commitment. However, she says their interaction that day showed her otherwise, shaking her faith in single fathers being willing or able to fully share their lives with her.

Parker says she empathizes with the single fathers' concerns about exposing their children to random women. She exercises some control when it comes to her own son, but says that when she's in a relationship she thinks it's important that her partner gets her son's approval. "My son is pretty independent. I allow him to speak his mind. When he meets a guy, he wants to know where he lives, what does he do, and, 'Why are you touching my mother?'"

Balancing her needs with the curiosity and concerns of her son often leaves her feeling alone. "I feel that sometimes I do get lonely, but I don't need to have a man." She does say that "at times it's convenient to have a relationship with someone to bounce ideas off of that's not a girlfriend." And she says men can also provide a release from the pressures of life, giving her a person to "lean on, talk to—that comfort zone so you don't have to deal with the single life." A significant other can also assist with making hard choices. Parker believes that "if I have that male figure in my home, I can ask questions or get direction in some sort of way."

Parker does not feel in need of direction right now, though, so she feels no need to rush into anything. She wants to make sure whatever man she selects is a good fit for her current family and life. She's clear that she's not looking for someone to take over her role either as a parent or a breadwinner. "It's kind of hard to get these young guys to understand that we can each have roles in the house," she says. Parker wants someone to share life with—someone who can create a positive partnership with her, who can add to the life she has masterfully crafted, not take away from it. "I would like to be married now because I am established. I want someone to balance me in some kind of way."

Until she finds someone who can meet her criteria, she says she'll continue to shore up her and her son's future and life. "I'm really trying to understand myself, because every relationship I've been in has been long-term." She wants to learn what she needs from a man that will add to the happiness she's achieved alone. In the meantime, she appreciates the simple comforts a man provides. "I miss rolling over and cuddling at night, doing things around the house that I don't have to rush and do.

I've been doing it for three years by myself, and I miss when he [my ex-boyfriend] used to help."

But Parker doesn't resent her role as full-time mother and father; in fact, her ability to do it all has shocked and amazed her. It's also changed her judgment about other women who are going through child-rearing alone. "I, myself, when I was in that situation I thought, 'Maybe this wasn't supposed to happen.'" But as time wore on, it occurred to her that you can say "maybe" until you are dead, and it wouldn't change anything. She says at that point, you have to continue living and carve out a new path to happiness for you and your child.

Parker thinks she has escaped the stigma attached to being a single mom by not surrounding herself or her child with a lot of men and by carrying herself with dignity and decency, traits that were enhanced by becoming a single mother. "Having my son made me stronger," she says, able to rise above the common notion and characteristics ascribed to a baby mama.

Part Three

Sex and the Single Sistah:
Dating In and Out of the Race

The sexuality of single black women is a topic that's been pondered throughout American history, arguably beginning with the creation of the "mammy" stereotype. At that point black females were seen as overweight, homely, and matronly and therefore too unattractive for their preferences or desires to even matter. One famous actress who epitomizes this typecasting is Academy Award winner Hattie McDaniel, best remembered for her performance in the film *Gone with the Wind*.

In the 1970s strongly negative images of black sexuality emerged. Blaxploitation films such as *Foxy Brown* and *Coffey* featuring actress Pam Grier showed confident, strong, sensual women. However, the characters she played were often also "angry black women," which is one of the most prevalent labels slapped on African American females to this day. It is that perceived uncontrollable fury that perpetuates the belief that black women are not the ideal relationship candidates.

During the same time period, if a black woman wasn't portrayed as angry, she was typecast as a perpetual victim. The record-breaking television miniseries *Roots*, from the book by Alex Haley, is one of the most prominent examples of this stereotype. Although it is a historical account of his own family's history, it is a story that resonated with generations of African Americans. But it also left the unshakable impression that black women have an overpowering sexuality that is irresistible to white men, thereby putting them at risk for being assaulted.

Unfortunately at present not much has changed to eradicate any of the previously held notions of black female sexuality. However, African American women are striving to change the narrative. The erotic fiction novels by authors like Zane and Carol Taylor showcase females of all shapes, sizes, and professions who are firmly in command of and acting on their desires.

A major shift has also come in terms of interracial dating. Statistics show that black women are no longer waiting for African American men to come to their senses. A growing number of black women are choosing to date outside of their race as a way to find a suitable mate. In 1960 there were only about twenty-six thousand couples consisting of a black wife and a white husband. However, since the Supreme Court changed the rules banning such unions, that number has more than quadrupled.

By choosing to pursue what makes them happy, be it dating outside their race or actively seeking out sexual partners, sistahs are defining their own happiness, hoping to change past perceptions by continuing to move forward and test boundaries.

7

Walking the Single's Beat

With Media Professional Kiada Moragne

"*Being alone doesn't bother me*, but being *labeled* alone is different; that implies something different than when I say it myself. It's like being called the n-word by a white person. I would, of course, say, 'Don't call me that,' but if I refer to myself as such, it's fine," says Kiada Moragne, a pint-sized spitfire who says she chose never to date seriously. The dreadlock-wearing Brooklyn native continues, "With me it's not what people think, because I could care less about that. It's just the negative connotation that's been attached to the word 'alone.'"

In fact the media professional hasn't gone without the company of a man. "I never had a problem getting what I want from a man, which was primarily sex, so I never have a problem being alone." She's chosen to have casual liaisons rather than messy entanglements. "I've never really had standards because I always went into it for the sex. I didn't take time to get into a relationship or get to know anybody. I just had sex and kept rolling. I didn't keep phone numbers or keep in contact unless I wanted sex with them again."

Acting on her pure animalistic instincts has provided Moragne with the physical comfort that she needs without taking her away from her professional or educational goals. "I know right off when I meet a man if I want to have sex with him, and I don't have time for all the nice-ties. We don't have to go out to dinner, he doesn't have to call me. I'm gonna just step up to him and tell him what I want. Let's make it real cut and dry."

Her lifestyle may evoke thoughts of not-so-flattering terms, like "slut," or its slang cousin "ho," both describing a woman who is sexually promiscuous. But Moragne says that while she's never had anyone call her names—at least not to her face—she knows the stigma attached to women who choose to be promiscuous. She has heard what people say about women perceived to have loose morals. In order to avoid judgment from others she acts discreetly. Still she insists she is not, nor would she ever be, ashamed of her lifestyle.

Moragne is open and honest about her past with men she meets. To those who choose to walk away, she says good riddance. However, she concedes that the children's rhyme that boasts that "sticks and stones may break my bones but words will never hurt me" is a fallacy, and any-one who's ever been on the receiving end of an unkind word knows it. Moragne insists she's strong enough to take whatever is dished out as it pertains to her lifestyle.

Moragne feels a kinship with popular singers such as Mariah Carey and Kelis, who have boldly expressed their sexuality, shouting out how proud they are that their feminine wiles drive men crazy. Their unabashed honesty about desire and pleasure is a window into the minds of sexually free women like Moragne, women who aren't doing anything with a man that they don't want to do.

Moragne says there is a clear distinction between women like herself and women who are with a man because they want something he can provide. Females like herself, and those depicted in lyrics by Carey and Kelis, select a person based on an actual desire to spend time with and enjoy another individual; it's a free situation where no one owes the other anything.

In her February 2008 release, "Touch My Body," Carey has no shame detailing what she wants from a man:

Touch my body
Put me on the floor
Wrestle me around
Play with me some more[1]

The 2003 hit "Milkshake" from Kelis further highlights the confidence that some women have in their prowess with men:

My milkshake brings all the boys to the yard,
And they're like, it's better than yours,
Damn right it's better than yours[2]

Many women identify with these lyrics and those who embody them. The truth is that a lot of women wish they'd lived their lives more like Moragne, at least if you believe Ariel Levy, the author of *Female Chauvinist Pigs: Women and the Rise of Raunch Culture*: "I think there are a lot of women who want to have a lot of sex because they enjoy it."[3] Some women would prefer to walk the single's beat their own way, regardless of what society thinks.

Ironically, the sexually liberated Moragne prefers more subtlety in her music. She's often heard belting out classic songs from Earth, Wind and Fire, the O'Jays, and the Whispers instead of the crude lyrics in some of today's popular music. Her attitude toward sex has also mellowed with age. Now that she's reached most of the individual goals she set for herself, Moragne no longer fears being distracted by a relationship. She's now free to spend the time and effort necessary to have a substantial connection with a man; a slower pace has allowed her to realize that she is ready to share more of her life. "I don't want to be an old maid. I want someone to lie in bed with at night. I don't want to go to bed alone all my life."

But she is aware that because she's not really had a deep connection with a man, she has a lot to learn when it comes to forming a lifetime partnership. "I'm not equipped to deal with a relationship. I have a very low tolerance, so I'm not equipped. I don't have a lot of patience; that's something you have to learn if you are going to be with anyone for a long period of time. So at thirty I'm trying to learn it, as opposed to people who have been in multiple relationships who already have it."

What Moragne has now is a willingness to let down her guard and let a man into her life. "I don't need a man to support me. Outside of sex you don't need a man to do much for you, but men do need to be needed. So sometimes you got to lean back and let them do things for you. If not, they don't feel adequate. If you can do everything, then they think 'What do you need me for?' So I can let go of some of my independence and let him do what he needs to do to feel like he's taking care of me."

This is quite a change for a woman who has been living on her own since she was in her late teens. She moved out of her mother's apartment when the two strong-willed women butted heads, though this fiercely outspoken and headstrong thirty-something didn't go far. She still lives in the same building as her mother, who is her greatest role model. Her mother, divorced with two daughters, raised them to be autonomous, and that's exactly what they are. Moragne put herself through both college and graduate school, earning a master's degree in criminal justice and remaining on the dean's list while working full-time at ABC television.

However, she has always kept a man on standby. "There was always someone in my life at some time. A guy was there on and off. When I was in school [college], I didn't have time to concentrate on nobody. It was the same with my undergraduate degree, school was my focus."

Moragne's current focus is her passion for law enforcement, a passion that is allowing her to take a twenty-thousand-dollar pay cut so she can enter the New York City Police Academy. According to the New York City Police Department Web site, only 17.4 percent of all cops are African American. "While I'm in the academy, I don't think I will have time for anything but getting out of there. When I am done, I would imagine I would have time to get out and mingle," she says.

After she makes officer, a husband is next up on the agenda. But that's only if a man can deal with her dangerous career. "If you want to be with me, you want to be here regardless of what I am doing. If you believe my career is a stipulation of you staying or going, I'm not going to give up my career because you don't like what I am doing. Then you got to go."

Brushing off anyone who doesn't agree with her vision for her life is something Moragne says she has no problem doing because her search for a partner is just beginning. "I always saw myself single at this age. I never saw myself having kids before my midthirties." Now she says, "My biological clock is ticking so I am slowing down."

She's also approaching motherhood as methodically as she approached her professional goals. "I think it is more difficult for women to conceive after forty, so I have to have kids soon." She's right—research shows that women over thirty-five have a higher likelihood of giving birth to a child with certain conditions, like Down syndrome. Studies also show that compared with women in their twenties, females from thirty-five to thirty-nine have double the risk of suffering a miscarriage. By the time women reach the ages of forty to forty-four, the danger skyrockets to about 50 percent.[4] Women over thirty-five are also more likely to have complications such as gestational diabetes, placental problems, premature delivery, and stillbirth.

After keeping herself abreast of the risks and rewards of having a child in her midthirties, Moragne decided, "I would prefer to have them

[kids] within a family." She says she wants someone to have her back in case something goes wrong and to help with the burdens of rearing the children should her new job as a cop put her at risk. "I don't want to be an old maid. I want to have a family and have kids, and I want to do that in the traditional way. But I want the kids primarily."

If she can't find a man in a short amount of time, she says she is willing to go it alone. "If it doesn't happen, if I don't find myself in a good relationship in a reasonable amount of time, I'll have the kids first and focus on a relationship later." She says she will do that by whatever means are available. "My focal point right now is having kids in a timely manner."

While she's willing to have a child out of wedlock, living with a man she's not married to is out of the question. "What am I going to live with you for? I can live by myself." She says if a man is willing to commit to having a child with her, then a ring shouldn't be that big of a stretch. "If I am going to have kids with someone, I'd rather be married than cohabitate and be a baby mama."

Moragne says living with a man and playing house would be settling for something she doesn't want. "No, I wouldn't settle. If I am settling then I can just have a boyfriend. A boyfriend is someone I'm not trying to marry, but he's there for a purpose."

In the end, she prefers to be a married mother of at least two children when all is said and done. She says she's going to be cautious about who she selects "because marriage is easy to get into but hard to get out of." A child of divorce herself whose sister has also been divorced but has since remarried, Moragne is aware of the pluses and minuses of building a life with someone, which is why she's held off for as long as she could. Now that she's developed the appropriate mindset for putting in the work that a marriage would take, she is ready to move forward.

The bright and determined future NYPD officer says, "I have no regrets about being single at this point in my life. I've had all the sex I could possibly want to have had. I've had all the men I wanted to have, and I'm still young enough to have a family." She says she's done "her thing," and now it's time to do the "family thing." "I'm in my thirties, I've gotten my education, made career moves, and I can still have time to have kids. I'm right on track as far as I am concerned." After all, she says, "Who wants a miserable ass woman who can't be comfortable by herself?"

8

Not All Black Women Are Angry

With Attorney and Professor Shenequa Grey

One of the most well-known and omnipresent African American stereotypes is that of the angry black woman. Black women have been caricatured in many ways, but, as Vanessa Jones points out in an article in the *Boston Globe*, "'This tart-tongued, neck rolling, loud-mouthed sister reigns on television."[1] And the perception that she's a realistic depiction of African American women has also invaded the lives of real-life, everyday ladies. "It's the workhorse," says Gail Wyatt, author of the acclaimed 1997 book on black female stereotypes *Stolen Women: Reclaiming Our Sexuality, Taking Back Our Lives*. According to her, there's a notion that every "black woman who's achievement-oriented, kind of no-nonsense, overworked, exhausted, is not particularly kind or compassionate but very driven."[2]

Attorney and professor Shenequa Grey says she's been confronted with the notion that she is just such a woman. "I've had people say, 'You are a little angry.' I don't think I am, but I am frustrated." Grey handles the assumption that she must be mad because she's still single; "I find myself giving a disclaimer. Sometimes the question comes straight out, and sometimes you can hear the tone in the conversation: 'Why aren't you married?' And, I have to say, 'I was engaged once.'"

Grey was betrothed to a man, but she made the painful decision to chase her individual career goals and accept an assistant district attorney's job in the Caddo Parish District Attorney's Office in Shreveport, Louisiana, rather than become a wife. She says, "I left an engagement in D.C. to come home and be a prosecutor, to go to the DA's office to further my career when my fiancé was saying he would like to go to a big city in New York or California. I definitely chose my career on several occasions over pursuing those relationships."

She is often irritated by the misperception that successful African American women like herself are angry merely because they are unmarried. She says there are so many other reasons for black women to be upset, a sentiment that's shared by Angela Burt-Murray, who cowrote *The Angry Woman's Guide to Life.* In it, Burt-Murray says there are different degrees of anger varying from productive to destructive. She chooses to embrace the positive side of black female anger. While she points out that there is a lot for African American women to be angry about, it's only when these females are able to harness that emotion that real change can happen. Burt-Murray cites historical figures such as Sojourner Truth, Rosa Parks, and Harriet Tubman as angry black women that have effected change in a productive manner.[3]

However, these women are not the standard image conjured up when one thinks of the angry black woman. Rather, it's of the reality stars such as Alicia Calloway on the 2001 installment of *Survivor: The Australian Outback*; Coral Smith, of MTV's *Real World/Road Rules Challenge*; and, most notably, Omarosa of *The Apprentice* fame. There was also been a movement to vilify Barack Obama's wife, Michelle, during the 2008 presidential campaign. Magazines like the *National Review*, programs on the Fox News Channel, and Web sites such as www.TheObamaFile.com depicted her as a disgruntled and unpatriotic woman. Michelle Obama said that she was proud of America for the first time in her adult life during the presidential race. Conservatives perceived this as a hostile swipe at the country rather than as a statement that reflects the sentiment held by many patriotic African Americans who have often felt disenfranchised. Yet the representation of her as an angry black woman became so prevalent that the *New Yorker* attempted to mock it in a now-infamous cover on which a drawing of her was outfitted like a Black Panther radical.

The problem is that the characterization of these women is so overpowering that the average black woman often finds herself lumped in and defined by their behavior, creating the attitude that she is not datable and certainly not marriage material. Jones says that to assume that all black women fit this stereotype is to not fully understand our complexity. She says some African American females are angry, but rightfully so. After being ignored, not taken seriously, and rejected, it's only natural. Nevertheless, Jones want to make it clear that she doesn't want to send the message that acting angry is the way black women should act.[4]

Shaking the idea that she is an angry black woman and not appealing to men isn't as simple as mentioning a former romantic entanglement, as Shenequa Grey does. The label is so engrained in popular culture that even the mainstream media frequently perpetuate it. It's so far reaching that former secretary of state Condoleezza Rice was branded with the angry black woman label when she first rose to power in the Bush administration. She was regularly shown in television and newspaper ads with a scowl on her face.

So it's no wonder that Grey, now an assistant professor of law at the Southern University Law Center in Baton Rouge, Louisiana, is finding it hard for men to look past her career achievements and see her as anything but an angry black woman who has it all, leaving some men feeling that there's nothing they can contribute to her life.

What Grey has been able to accomplish is impressive. According to the 2000 U.S. Census, only 28.7 percent of all lawyers are women, with just 1.9 percent of them being African American; this makes her one of merely 16,415 black female attorneys nationwide. However, for a woman featured in the *Ebony* magazine article "Super Single Sisters of 2002," being single more than seven years later has left her with a feeling of exasperation that the quality of men she's met in the last six years hasn't improved.

She says that if she isn't dating a man who feels intimidated by her, she meets men who have equal education and professional success but believe they have so many options there's no reason for them to settle down. Grey is often asked by men, "Why are so many women angry and what are they angry about?"—questions she says she almost never answers. She claims the answers to these questions are obvious; that women, like her, are frequently disappointed by the caliber of men they date because the men don't see these successful women as equals. Grey says she's worked too hard to excel in her career to be relegated to taking a backseat to her mate in order to boost his ego and make him comfortable with her level of success.

She says, "There are a lot of African American men who are educated and have decent jobs, and they are very much a commodity. They realize that, and they are being more selective and waiting a lot longer to get married." It's given black men a cockiness that's made them believe they can have anything they want from a woman without any of the responsibility. "I feel like there are some African American men who are very happy and pleased to not have to take on that responsibility in a society where they don't feel they need to. You've got a family, you have to work. You have to use some of your money for your wife and children and not buy cars and rims and all this type of stuff."

Grey says all men aren't this blatant about their unwillingness to assume what they see as the burden of a family. For a lot of African American men, they just don't really feel there is a need to be saddled with only one woman. "That's part of a survey that I did myself. I asked African American men whether or not they believe that there is anything that they are missing—if there are any benefits that they are not getting by not being married—and most of them said no."

She's quick to point out that men aren't solely to blame for feeling like they don't need to settle down to have everything they want. "There is a lot of responsibility black women have to take for being in this position, for staying in relationships with these guys for seven and eight years and having kids for the same [person] or multiple people. Once a person has demonstrated that they are not really interested in being with you, you have to let them go. But there are certain people who feel like it's better than being alone or believe 'a piece of a man is better than no man.'" She believes that staying in a unfulfilling relationship is a weakness that she doesn't have. But she's aware that not all women share her sense of self-belief, so it's hard for them to imagine not having a man by their side and being happy.

Grey believes this need for a connection with a man is sometimes expressed through promiscuity. She thinks sexual freedom on the part of women is another contributor to the disconnection between men and women when it comes to forming a family unit. She says that ever since the 1960s and the introduction of birth control, women have been more lax about whom they go to bed with; this, she says "has had an effect in both races, although it has been a lot more significant in the African American race. There does seem to be a lot of casual sex going on more than at the time of our parents." While she does not claim to be a virgin, sharing herself with a multitude of men isn't something she chooses to do. Instead, Grey would rather wait for a man who satisfies her intellectually and spiritually before giving herself physically.

She says women have allowed themselves to become sex objects rather than full human beings with a variety of needs. Men are just taking advantage of the opportunity. "Since the sexual revolution, men feel like they can get 'all the milk for free.' The 'why buy the cow when you can get all the milk you want for free' syndrome. Women are having a lot of casual sex. Men can get it as much as they want. With successful women outnumbering men, they have a lot of choices so they just go down the list to the next few that they have. So, a lot of black men don't have an incentive to get married. They have children so they aren't worried about that. They know that if you start talking about commitments and relationships that they don't want, they can go on and be with other women who are not 'pressuring' them." She says women hold the power; they have the ability to change men's attitudes. "It really is up to the woman for herself and for other women to start setting higher standards so that men can't run around and get everything they want for free." Grey does just that, choosing to abstain until she feels she has a real connection with a man; a practice that shrinks her dating pool but allows her to maintain her self respect.

She points out that women should be aware that sex is never free; it comes with real emotional and possibly deadly physical consequences. Besides regaining the reverence of men and possibly stemming the disintegration of the black family, Grey says there are more serious reasons for black women to cut down on casual sex. "When you look at the statistics, at the rate that black women are being exposed to HIV and other sexually transmitted diseases, 49 percent of diagnosed cases in 2005, black women were twenty-three times more likely to get certain STDs, not to mention we have so many children being born out of wedlock. We have to look at black men being the primary cause of why black women are being exposed to these things. It stems from men having multiple sex partners and having unprotected sex." She's right, as statistics show. Of all African Americans diagnosed with AIDS in 2006, 36 percent of them were women.[5] In fact, black women accounted for 66 percent of all women diagnosed with AIDS that year.[6] The rate of infection, combined with the disparity in health care access, is blamed for AIDS now being the leading cause of death for black women ages twenty-five to thirty-four.[7]

Grey points out that in addition to saving themselves from potential health risks, women should consider that one of their main motivations for sleeping with various men is often a falsehood. "Women in some cases are having sex for enjoyment, but in other cases they are trying to compete for men, trying to up their game." She continues that "you can have all the sex you want; it's still not going to make him marry you if he doesn't want to." Grey believes it's important that women have enough confidence to have sex on their own terms, not to gain the admiration of a man. She says doing so will prevent women from feeling that if they don't or can't keep a man, they are missing something in their lives.

Grey says the same goes for women who live with or remain with a man without a ring. She claims these women use "play marriages" to try to obtain the emotional security that comes along with the real thing. "It's a long-term commitment, saying that 'I really want to be here for as long as I am here.' A lot goes along with that." She says that by not getting a commitment from a man, women are often relegated to lives racked with financial drawbacks they wouldn't have if married. "You start to pool your resources; you buy a home together; you share money—a lot of things that if you are single and living together you have reservations about doing." By not seeking the relationship they really want, Grey asserts that these women are making themselves human doormats, allowing men to control their life and destiny.

She points out that women often complicate things further when they choose to have children with men they aren't bound to legally. "I would not feel comfortable having a child with a man who doesn't want to marry me. I would be thinking: 'This man wants to be able to maintain his freedom so he could leave.'" She says unless women are really OK with being a single parent, they should take a long, hard look at their mate. "Personally, I wouldn't like to raise a child without his or her father in their life because it is a huge responsibility. It takes more than one person to raise a child."

Grey believes a lot of black woman have children out of wedlock because they believe it will help them keep their man. But, she says, conversations she's had with men indicate that babies aren't the key to keeping their attention. She says men often tell her that they want more—women who give them total freedom, who say little about whatever it is they choose to do with their lives. Moreover, she says they tell her that if black women were serious about not being alone they'd stop complaining and do more to keep their men.

She says the "more" black men are referring to is simply code. "Within that 'more,' they mean more sexual favors, so they are basically using black women. They have black women thinking they can get a man like that, so 'I can keep having sex with him for three or four years and when he is finally ready to get married, he'll choose me.'"

Despite this, she says, black men are increasingly turning their backs on sistahs, opting to date and marry females of other races regardless of the relatively low standards set by many black women. Statistics indicate that about three-quarters of the 403,000 black-white interracial couples in the United States in 2006 contained African American husbands; that's nearly four times the reverse involving black women and white men.[8] "I think it's interesting that a lot of black men date other races, but they have a problem with black women dating outside their race. Black women are pretty loyal, for the most part, about dating black men, but broadening our options is something we should consider," Grey contends. It appears that a greater proportion of African American women are doing just that. In 2006 the U.S. Census showed that there were 117,000 black wife–white husband couples; that's up by 22,000 from 2000.[9]

Grey says black men don't like it when the shoe is on the other foot—when black women follow their lead across racial dating lines. "I call that the interracial double standard. They definitely explore any option that they want—you know, Italian, Latino, Asian—but they don't want to see that from black women, and they do consider it a slap in the face. At some point, we have to realize that we can't let black men control our actions and thoughts, because they're doing whatever they want to do." She says black women have to be bold enough to pursue their happiness despite the reaction of black men. "I've had conversations with black men who said they don't want a woman coming back to them after she's been over there. At the same time, we've given them more than enough opportunity to be here, but they probably weren't going to be here anyway."

She says she's worn out by the unwillingness of black men to step up to the plate. Grey has forced herself to reevaluate her own thoughts on interracial dating. "For many years I had been adamantly saying I wanted to date and marry a black man, but that hasn't worked out." Now she has torn down the walls, choosing to date a man of any race that values her mind, career, and family values.

Hollywood took on the topic of black women dating white men in the 2006 romantic film *Something New*, starring Sanaa Lathan and Simon Baker. In it, Kenya McQueen, played by Lathan, is a CPA who is in desperate need of a date. She hires a white landscaper to work on the backyard at her newly purchased ranch home and develops a relationship with him. Still, she is resistant to the suggestion that her fling with him was anything but just that. So she dumps him, opting to go out with a black attorney played by actor Blair Underwood. While she feels nothing for Underwood, Lathan's character feels a sense of loyalty to her race so continues to stick with him until she's overwhelmed by her feeling for Baker's character. The culmination of the movie is when Lathan's character overcomes her shame, at the urging of her father, and brings Baker's character to a black society event. The struggle that Lathan's character goes through is the same pain and agonizing pressure many black women feel before they decide to date outside of their race.

Grey says that black women are getting over this pressure. In response to the decrease in partners and the vast opportunities now available to people of color, "I know that black women are also certainly educating themselves at a higher rate than we were back in those days and being self-sufficient. We do not have to marry to find a good man or marry to have someone to take care of us. We're in a position where we can say, 'I'm going to find someone who I am attracted to, who I am compatible with, and all these sorts of things.'"

No matter what she accomplishes in the business arena, having a functioning relationship is still important to her. "I do think it's normal. Personally, that is what I believe—that we are put on this earth to be companionship for each other and to procreate." She goes on to say, "I think, at the end of the day, it is something that is very natural, and people wonder 'What is the problem that you're not married?' even though we may have said that's not going to happen and we've moved on."

Grey asserts that to avoid wasting time while searching for a man, you have to follow your other dreams and refuse to settle for an inadequate relationship. "I remember my mother always giving me two pieces of advice: 'Get your education' and 'Don't marry a man you don't love,'" which is something she certainly won't do. But she is quick to point out that often women are thought to be settling when they've just changed their criteria for a partner. "There are some women who are able to settle, and some who are not. I always feel like, for a lot of women, their standards change. As they get older, they might appear to be settling, but in reality the man has changed into what they value at that time."

For her, she says any potential husband will have to add to her present happiness, not detract from it. "At the end of the day, I have to be happy with the man that I am with. I want to be attracted to him. I want to want to do things for him, to kiss him when he comes home. I don't want to be thinking, 'Oh my goodness, he's home. I got to be dealing with him all night.'"

Her life doesn't leave any room for dealing with someone who isn't worth it. Grey has built a career making a difference in the lives of the most downtrodden in society. As assistant district attorney, she has prosecuted sex offenses and violent crime cases, including those involving rape, armed robbery, and murder. Now she shapes young minds, teaching them about criminal procedure, torts, agency and partnership, and trial advocacy. This is not to say that should the right man come along she won't free up the time to be with him.

Having a family is important to Grey, whose parents have both passed on. Although she has two brothers, she says they have their own families in other cities, leaving her a virtual orphan in Louisiana. "I certainly want to get married and have children. If I left here without having those things, I would feel that that was a part of my life I missed out on." So she's willing to take steps as a single woman to ensure she has the part of her dreams she can control. "In the next four or five years, I would consider other options to have a kid. At this point, I don't even have my parents. I don't want to die alone and not have children. That much I can control, so I would definitely look into other options."

Regardless of which path she ends up taking, with or without a man, Grey is clear that she's at peace with her place in life. "I'm happy right now being single. I don't know how long I am going to be happy, but it is possible, if you have truly found things that are fulfilling for you." Grey has done just that, finding joy in what she does rather than finding fault with her life for what she doesn't have.

9

Even a Broken Clock Is Right Twice a Day

With Movie Producer Effie T. Brown

"*Different*"—*that's the word* that movie producer Effie T. Brown uses to describe herself. From her fiery red dreads to her brown skin and her curvaceous figure, she's definitely not run of the mill in Hollywood. Her external and creative anomalies have allowed her to stand out in what tends to be a formulaic industry. They are also what make her stand out in her private life, especially when it comes to the common expectation that all women have a biological clock.

"Kids personally frighten me. I'm thirty-five. Aren't we supposed to feel our biological clock kick in by now? Well, I don't have that." She continues, "I think kids are cute, but I'm like 'take it or leave it.' I have no strong desire to reproduce. I mentor. I definitely want to spread whatever message or whatever little knowledge I have to my fellow sisters out there, but that's about it."

This lack of a maternal instinct and the lack of a man on her arm draw frequent fire from other people, including her own family. "People, my family, are always saying things like, 'Is she's gay? She's gay.' No, I'm not gay. Not that there is anything wrong with being gay. I just don't have a man." She says giving that answer only prompts more questions and comments, like: "Why don't you have a man?" "She must be a gold digger." "For her to have somebody, a man must have to be where she is or have more than she does for it to work."

Brown says people are completely wrong when it comes to money being an issue in her choosing a man. She says a potential mate just has to be on board with her plan for her life. "I had certain goals—like by the time I was thirty, I wanted to have a house, and I've got my house. That's one of the things that was important to me. . . . Now, I want a house in Portland or New York, and a man has be down with that. If not, oh well, you're not the guy for me."

Anyone who wants to be with Brown would have to understand that she's had to work hard and stay confident in order to be taken seriously in the movie business. Her dedication and success have drawn the interest of various industry publications. In a 2005 interview with FilmMonthly.com, she discusses what it's like to be both black and a woman, often breaking new ground and not always certain what the outcome will be. She commented, "What I find amazing is that when I am traveling around making movies, I never get to forget that I'm black and a woman, not that I would ever be anything else. I'm like: 'Right! You're from a small town and have never had to deal with a woman of color in a position of authority.' You know you have to keep your cool and see things from their perspective."[1]

Being a maverick in the true sense of the word and being able to produce films that illustrate her insight into the plight of the underdog is how Brown made a name for herself. She uses her ability to think outside of the box to make decisions to pick up the phone and take risks that many would not. Just before graduating from Loyola Marymount college in 1993, she called Loretha Jones, a contact she'd made through the Black Business Connection.[2] Before she knew it, Brown had a rare opportunity. She was given a production job on the Robert Townsend movie *The Five Heartbeats*. Working on that movie led to more projects, which helped Brown make the decision to form her full-service production company in 2001.[3] The work of her company, Duly Noted, Inc., helped Brown earn the Motorola Producer Award at the 2003 Independent Spirit Awards.

Brown's breakthrough in the film industry came with the release of *Real Women Have Curves.* The movie, which she produced, was the winner of the Dramatic Audience Award at the 2002 Sundance Film Festival. The film chronicles the coming of age of Ana, a first generation Mexican American. Brilliantly played by America Ferrara, now of television's *Ugly Betty* fame, the story follows Ana as she has to choose between family obligations and a full scholarship to Columbia University.

Real Women Have Curves was just the jumping-off point for Brown, who has since released the movie *Rocket Science* in 2007. She's now working on eight more films due out in the next three to five years, including *Bobby Zero,* starring actor/rapper Mos Def. Quite an accomplishment for an army brat who turned her fifty-thousand-dollar investment into a company that grossed about six million dollars in 2007. Brown's motto is "Give us five million and we'll give you a badass movie."[4]

What may not be apparent about this fiercely driven New Jersey native who devised an innovative way to the top of her craft is that her unique perspective on relationships has little to do with the example she got from her parents. In fact, the rebel comes from a conventional background. "My parents are still together, they've been married for forty-something years, they love each other. I had fantastic relationships in my life." Still, she says, her mother was the one who helped instill and support her perspective about not being dependent on marriage. Brown's mother also wasn't critical about her pronouncement that she didn't want to have children. "From the very beginning my mother told me that being by yourself or being alone and being lonely are two very different things. Being independent is about having the strength to walk the road alone. Thank God for her putting that in my head at an early age. It guides me now."

Brown's independent streak also mirrors the spirit of her grand-mother, for whom she is named. "My grandmother is Big Effie; I'm little Effie. Her husband died a few years ago. In the last five or six years, my aunt got married, and my grandmother said, 'You know, Effie, there's nothing wrong with being by yourself. You know there's nothing wrong with that. You don't have to go and try to get married.' She said, 'If I were your age now, in this day and age, I wouldn't have gotten married.' That flipped me out."

Brown also says that although it may not be overtly apparent, society has changed, along with women's attitudes about their futures. "Back in the day, people got married earlier so they went from their parents house to their married house, but we've been in our own houses for so long, it's like, 'What do you mean we have to share space?'" Women today also have more financial security, which she says has allowed women to be more selective about a mate. "You don't have to be attached to a man to make ends meet. You don't have to. You should be with somebody because you want to, not because you have to."

Brown says that while she relishes the freedom that comes with "sin-gledom" and not having children, she says there are also some down-sides. "Sunday mornings—that's when I miss it [having a boyfriend] the most. When you're like, 'It would be great to have breakfast, read the paper, some morning nookie—that would be great.'" She says her circle of friends shares the same notion, but they've all vowed to enjoy their lives should they find themselves waking up alone indefinitely. "I'd love to have a boyfriend or husband; that would be great. A lot of my girl-friends are single so we talk about it, but we'll be damned if we come at it as if our lives aren't fabulous just because we don't have men."

She admits that there is a drawback to aging alone: wondering who will be there to take care of you. "There is a whole method to the mad-ness of it all—why people are having children and why they're getting married young. It's the cycle of life. You get to a certain point, and your kids are able to take care of you. I am breaking that cycle." Keeping that in mind, Brown is making provisions to ensure the security of both her and her parents whether or not there is the assistance of offspring. "I have the potential of not having that, so I have to make sure that while I am healthy I keep myself together, get my retirement plan together."

To make her retirement dream a reality, Brown is saving her pennies; something a recent survey by Argosy Research for Ariel Mutual Funds and Charles Schwab Corporation found the average black person does not do. African Americans are saving less for retirement than whites, and close to half of them avoid the stock market. In fact, "on average, savings for black Americans earning $50,000 or more a year is $48,000, compared with $100,000 for whites with the same income and educational background."[5] But, Brown made it clear that she is aware of how much it would take for her to be comfortable once she stops working full-time. She's also got her parents' best interests at heart. "My parents, as long as there is breath in me, are going to be taken care of." Being single, she knows the weight of being financially responsible for herself and them rests squarely on her.

It's clear that Brown's eye is on her family, her work, and her future, factors she believes could have a lot to do with her current single status. "I've always been ambitious in a more career-minded kind of way." But she believes that if she is supposed to have a relationship with a man, a higher power will guide that person to her and make it easier for her to make room for him in her life. A relationship is "a gift from God; it's not anything I can control. If it happens, it happens. If it doesn't, it's not the end all and be all. I think that's why I always focused on career, because that's something I could physically change by being dedicated to reach the goal and to reach an end."

She also thinks that since she's never been in a relationship that's driven her to want a diamond ring, she has yet to feel she's missing something. "You desire for something when you've had a taste of it. It's a little

Buddhist, but that's the cause of suffering. It's when you've had something, and you can't have it again, then you begin to obsess over it. I've never had something like, 'This is the guy that I want to spend my life with,' so I don't really have any regrets." As she said earlier, occasionally she does miss male companionship. "I've had a boyfriend, so I miss that, but it's not something that will drive me to the point of distraction."

Refusing to be deterred from her goals may be why Brown says she is happy with her place in life. "I've been focused on wanting to be a successful producer, and that's something I want, and that's a struggle." It's a fight she is willing to wage so that she can feed her soul, make films that add to the social dialogue, and, of course, add to her bank account. "Five years from now when I am forty, I hope that I am the woman, the human being, I always wanted to be. In ten years, the plan is that I am more financially stable because I want to retire."

Like all good Hollywood love stories, Brown is not opposed to having a man as part of her happy ending. "God willing, my Mr. Right comes in. I do believe it will be unconventional. I don't believe I have any qualms with us having separate bedrooms." She says that way she and her partner can both have their space but spend time together when they choose.

In the meantime she will continue to blaze her own path to having a future that's complete, even if that means her personal movie will fade to black without a leading man. "I'm definitely open to being knocked off my feet. But I'm not actively biting my nails waiting for it."

Part Four

Rewriting the Fairy Tale

As a girl in the seventies and eighties, I, like millions of other girls, drifted off to sleep with a book filled with princess stories resting on my chest. Most of them took me to faraway lands where a poor, lonely, young girl could be swept up in adventure by rich, handsome, and charming men. These characters, like Cinderella, Sleeping Beauty, and Snow White, always found a lasting connection with their saviors; a bond that was destined to last forever. At the time I didn't understand the word "forever," but what I did know was that I, too, wanted the kind of love that could snatch me from the jaws of death and despair.

Of course, as girl I couldn't articulate my want for a "perfect man," one that would fill my every need and desire. I also wasn't conscious of how the effect of these fairy tales resonated in my life, especially when it came to my choice of mate or to determining whether or not to remain in a relationship. I suspect other women weren't—and aren't—aware as well.

The first time it occurred to me that perhaps there is no such thing as "happily ever after" was when I lost my first love. Never in any of the stories I read in my youth did Prince Charming say "I love you" and then take it back, leaving the princess to fend for herself.

That jolt to my reality wasn't welcomed at the time, but losing the fantasy of the perfect man has released me from the unrealistic expectations. It allows me to write my own fairy-tale ending; one that releases me from a holding pattern that requires me to wait for a man to rescue me from my life. Truth be told, I don't need nor want to be saved from my life, and neither do many other women. We like who we are, we're proud of what we've achieved, and we want a partner only if he can accept us as we are and share in our lives.

This may not be the fairy tale of old, but it is a version that has a real possibility of coming true.

10

Happily Ever After?

With Publisher, Literary Agent, and Book Distributor Nancey Flowers

Sleeping Beauty and Cinderella got their happy endings. Nearly every woman depicted on the silver screen has gotten her perfect partner, too, even in gut-wrenching stories like *Monster's Ball*. So it was only natural for Nancey Flowers to think she'd found her "real life" prince. After all, the Morgan State University graduate married her high school sweetheart after four years together. Unlike a film that ends in two hours, actual relationships last much longer and often don't play out like well-crafted scripts. "I expected to have the house, children, et cetera," she says. "I have the house, but no children. Things didn't go as planned, but that's simply a part of life. You pick up the pieces and keep it moving."

Flowers kept going by getting past the hard part, the divorce. "By 2001 we were separated and divorced in 2004. It was a sad moment in time for me, and deep down I wish things didn't have to end, but he was no longer respectful of our vows and we had to part ways." She also evaluated what went wrong between them. "My career played a part in my divorce. However, if I had to say what percentage, the erosion would be ten percent. The other ninety percent was issues we failed to overcome and simply gave up on."

She hasn't given up on finding someone to build a life with despite the poor outcome of her previous marriage. "I know that I will get married again. I won't sell myself short or involve myself in a relationship destined for Nowhere, USA!" She's even optimistic about the person she's involved with now. "I'm in a newfound relationship and hope to see this move to the next level, which is marriage."

On the surface it would seem that being with a man is an essential component to her happiness, but Flowers makes a point to state that a relationship is not everything. "I don't regret being single, but I enjoyed being married. It's better and healthier, if you're fortunate enough to find the right person."

Minus a fitting partner, Flowers says she's grown into herself. "I'm capable of doing a lot more than I give myself credit for. I'm a very ambitious person, and during my first marriage I was very reserved. Now I'm aggressive and wear many hats. I work a nine-to-five; I have a publishing company, literary agency, a book distribution company; and I also do marketing consulting if my schedule permits. If I were married, I wouldn't be able to do quite as much, but that's a sacrifice I'm willing to make." But she believes that a real fairy-tale ending doesn't involve her trading her career for family. "I don't believe you have to sacrifice one for the other."

Nor does she feel that she's being less of an independent-minded career woman by admitting that she'd like to share her life with a man. "Who doesn't want to be loved? Have a steady companion for trips, dates, and to lie around the house with. Dream big with, share fantasies with, raise a family with. Grow old with, laugh with, cry with, share a meal with—and split the mortgage with."

But Flowers is not judgmental about women who don't feel as she does. "Some people simply opt to remain single, and that's their prerogative. Others simply haven't found the right person." She believes she is the latter. But she does not consider herself alone, least of all lonely, without a permanent mate. "I don't consider myself lonely. However, I do realize that in order to complete the equation a man is required." Her spirituality tells her that God did not put us on this earth to be alone. "I strongly believe that in order to build strong communities, we need each other to survive. It takes a village to raise a child and a family."

While she'd prefer to have a child with a man she loves, motherhood is not something Flowers says she'd forgo if her Prince Charming doesn't come along. However, she does have restrictions on how she'd go about it. She refuses to consider sperm donation or out-of-wedlock pregnancy as alternatives. She says, "Adoption is an option, but I won't go through child bearing alone."

Nonetheless, Flowers is conflicted between her desire to be a mother and the notion that she, or any woman, could successfully raise a child alone. She thinks that vital job is better done as a two-person unit. "The concept that we women can do everything by ourselves holds some truth, but at the end of the day, how complete are we? Our children are more wayward now than ever, and it can truly be linked to single-parent households. While we're busy smashing the glass ceiling and blazing trails, we leave our children to be raised by misogynistic programming, biased media, ignorant and misinformed people on the streets, and individuals who just don't have the best intentions for our future. We can't do everything, at least it's not the natural order of things."

To Flowers it's natural for a woman to want someone to help with the burdens and blessings in life, such as children, home care, and so on. She believes it's part of the normal evolution of a loving union between two people. "Is it too much to ask for, that the man that I choose to be with respect me enough to place a ring on my finger? It was only forty years ago when cohabitating was frowned upon. In order to live with someone, you got married first. There was a place where just about every family had both parents present, even if they did bicker; they still had each other." She says it was "a time when we'd say proudly, 'No matter what goes down, blood is thicker than water.' But family values have gone down the drain. The bottom line is I want to build a family, and to me that requires marriage. Is happiness guaranteed? No! Life offers no guarantees."

Being divorced, Flowers says she knows that marriage is no promise of an endless connection. "Being married has its upside and downside. But if you're clever you'll have more ups than downs." She says she's learned that a way to ensure longevity is by not sweating the small stuff and by focusing on the big picture. "Why argue over the smallest things that won't change your tomorrow? Worry about things that will impact the marriage over the course of the years. If you believe you'll forget about it by end of the day or the following day, is it really worth the effort of fighting? Your partner should ultimately be your best friend, and that's what you gain by having a husband."

Her opinions may in part be shaped by her view of her mother's life as empty, outside of her children. "I look at my mother who has been a widow for over twenty-five years. She remained single while raising her four daughters, because she feared a man would try to molest or bring harm to us. I respect her for that decision. However, she's still alone, and her constant companions are the cat and her best friend who lives in the vicinity. She's financially sound, but she's alone. Money can buy you items and on occasion people, but not honest and true companionship."

Flowers's attitude about money not being the root of happiness explains why she doesn't require a man to have the same earning potential as she does. "Is it fair that a woman be on the same level as a man as far as success, money, et cetera? We live in such a unisex society that many women find themselves competing with their mates. I don't believe it matters who makes more than whom. However, if the woman makes more, it could create insecurities with the man. He may have issues, and you either work through them or decide early on that this isn't going to work before you jump the broom."

Avoiding another divorce is high on her agenda. Flowers is hoping her next marriage is her last because she finds that doing everything on her own has been taxing. "Being single is not easy . . . However, don't sell yourself short; if you're going to get involved with someone, they should cherish, respect, and learn to love you for who you are." She thinks part of the reason more women find themselves floundering in the dating scene is that they give away their bodies and souls to men who have no intentions of taking them seriously.

She comments, "As women, we've allowed ourselves to become too accessible to men. Men no longer feel that they have to commit because women practically throw themselves at men. It's common for women to have a one night stand now," She believes that women are not being discriminating enough about the men they choose to have relations with, often giving themselves to men who don't respect them or treat them well simply to have someone next to them at night.

Sexual liberation isn't the only factor she cites for men's lackadaisical attitude toward getting into and staying faithful within a marriage. She says some women's willingness to get involved with married men is a problem. Flowers says women should "respect [themselves] enough to walk away from a man who says that he's involved, married or otherwise. It's not worth it, and if you are able to take him away from that woman, just imagine how easy it'll be for another woman to snatch him away from you!"

She says the most important rule women can follow in terms of ensuring their happiness and that of others is to "respect yourselves and your fellow women friends." By doing that, females can be happy with themselves and their lives no matter what their relationship status. She's certainly following her own advice so that she can achieve her happily ever after this time around.

11

Singular Sensation

With Interior Designer Sheila Bridges

Turning houses into homes and offices into oases is how Sheila Bridges achieved fame. She amassed her fortune by building a reputation as the go-to interior designer for celebrities, including music mogul Sean Combs, author Tom Clancy, and Motown president Andre Harrell. But it is her work for her Harlem neighbor, President Bill Clinton, that has catapulted her into the designing stratosphere. Named America's Best Designer by *Time* magazine and CNN, she is accustomed to being in demand professionally, but limited in the time she has for her dating life.

"For me, my twenties were very, very social. My focus probably had more to do with my relationships/boyfriends at the time. Then a few light bulbs started to go on about what I wanted to do with my life, and things shifted. My thirties came along, and it became about discovering what I was passionate about, and I started my business."

In 1994 the Pennsylvania native opened Sheila Bridges Designs, and her work consistently put her on *House Beautiful*'s list of the country's top one hundred interior designers. The Brown University and Parsons School of Design graduate says most everything she imagines has come true, proving that she's a woman who can get what she wants when she puts her mind to it. "I visualized all sorts of things: myself riding horses, having a home, having a dog, having a business, traveling around the world. I created a picture in my mind and my heart, and many of those things I have achieved." She says she didn't have that same visualization when it came to relationships. "I've had so many friends over the years that had a vision of walking down the aisle in the white gown—what the dress would look like, sketching it out—but I never had that. I just never saw that, maybe that's why it never materialized."

What did materialize was a thirteen-acre property in upstate New York complete with a nineteenth-century colonial home so she could enjoy the great outdoors by hiking, snowboarding, and horseback riding. It also wasn't long before her talent led her to open a home furnishings store. Her passion for writing and design led her to craft the book: *Furnishing Fast Forward: A Practical Guide for Furnishing for a Lifetime.* She also had a television show, *Sheila Bridges Designer Living,* which lasted four seasons. Between all of that there were regular appearances on other programs like NBC's *Today Show* and *Oprah* and articles in numerous magazines. Bridges soon found her work environment not conducive to dating. "I realized that I was unlike a lot of people who may work in a corporate environment, commute to work, or work for big organizations, as they come in contact with different people all the time."

Bridges works out of a landmark Harlem apartment that she moved into in 1993. Since that time the seven-room space with a breathtaking view of the historic New York neighborhood has been featured in scores of publications. "My office is my home. I really have to remind myself that I can't always get so comfortable in that environment—that if I am invited to a party or social event, I really should make the effort to go out."

Bridges says that both her age and success level have fostered a shift in attitude, changing from focusing almost exclusively on her career to making herself more available to date. "I think now I am making a more conscious effort than I used to and I believe it's a function of where I am professionally in my life." As she has with her business ventures, Bridges feels that it's up to her to change the course of her life. "If you do want a relationship or if you do want to eventually get married or have a partner, you have to take some responsibility for it in that you have to make it important on a certain level."

Still, she makes it clear she is happy with her life the way it is right now. "My life is very full and very rich. I'm alone in terms of the status of obviously not being married, but I have a very important sense of connectedness to close friends and family and other people. So I guess I don't feel that I am alone." She says that despite this, she knows that single people are often seen as lonely or sad no matter what they have accomplished. "I always think when you look at someone like Oprah Winfrey, who is the pinnacle of success and what she has achieved, there are still people who feel sorry for her. They are like 'Oh, she's not married.' Unfortunately, society doesn't distinguish between being alone and being lonely. They are two completely different things."

The distinction is important for women in particular to understand. "As women, our value is somehow always contingent on or defined by our relationship with a man." But Bridges points out that "being alone is not a static sort of state. It doesn't mean you'll forever be alone." And she says there's no reason not to be happy while alone. She says it's imperative that women get to know themselves both inside and outside of a relationship. "At some point, most women are going to experience being alone. It may be that you married and got divorced. It may be that you had a partner, and he or she died. It may be that you never got married. It's a really good idea to feel comfortable by yourself to get to know *you*." Bridges cautions that women who do not have a good sense of themselves could end up in a situation worse than being single. "There are a lot of people in relationships just for their [the relationships'] sake. Just because people are in relationships doesn't mean that they're happy. It doesn't mean their relationships are positive and supportive."

So what is she looking for in a potential mate? Bridges makes it clear that she rebuffs the common expectation that a man must have the same monetary or social standing. "I don't want to date the male version of me. I just want to be with somebody I want to be with. I really want a man who is passionate about what he does. That could be a doctor or a carpenter. Whatever the job is, as long as he is passionate about what he does, that is attractive to me. It has less to do with the money."

She also says a child from a man's previous relationship isn't a deterrent either. "When I was in my thirties, I never considered dating men who had kids. That shifted and, in fact, more of the men I have dated have kids."

The seemingly fearless entrepreneur does have a limit to what she will take on alone. "It's a no-brainer for me that if I don't have a husband, then I won't have kids." Bridges says her traditional upbringing is a key factor in her being leery of becoming a single parent. "A lot of people ask me about having a baby on my own. Because I grew up in a two-parent household, I can't separate being married from being a family." She says that while she chose to embrace the responsibility for her career alone, children are a totally different matter. "I wanted to do it on my own in terms of taking risks in my professional life, but I am not comfortable with doing that on my own as a single woman by becoming a single parent."

Since 2004, Bridges faced multiple enormous challenges alone: the end of her TV show, the severing of her Achilles tendon, her mother's heart attack, and her father's diagnosis of Alzheimer's disease. As if all of this weren't enough, Bridges was also diagnosed with alopecia areata, an autoimmune disease that causes hair loss. At that point the glare of the spotlight became painful for her. She closed her Madison Avenue office and retreated back to her Harlem home, relying on her friends and family to get her through the tough times. "Some people thought I was sick or that I was going through chemotherapy or simply trying to make a bold fashion statement . . . that bothered me, but as with everything, you make the best of what you have, and you keep moving."[1]

She talked about the pain and havoc the condition initially wreaked on her self-esteem in a November 2007 interview with *Ebony* magazine. "I've had to dig deeply to redefine my feelings and ideas about beauty because otherwise, if I had to base it on the feedback I get from people of society, my life would be horrible." Her life has been anything but horrible, possibly because Bridges has refused to succumb to public pressure to cover her scalp by wearing a wig. In that same interview she said, "I had to be able to heal from the inside out. I felt like a wig was like a mask. I needed to be able to look myself squarely in the eye in the mirror every day and like what I saw."[2]

Instead of focusing on her appearance, she's turned her attention to the spiritual and emotional growth she's gained from her adversity. *Essence* magazine recognized her inspirational change by naming her one of the world's twenty-five most inspiring women in a 2006 article. In the spread, subtitled "Bold and Beautiful," Bridges posed proudly showing off her baldness. After that, articles with her displaying her hairless beauty began popping up everywhere, including *O* magazine and *O at Home*.

Bridges is just as focused as ever on what she deems important. She's unveiled a Harlem Toile bedding line and has released an outdoor furniture collection. She's also launched a newsletter called *The Nestmaker* so her fans can interact with her. Further, Bridges has decided to take on fewer design jobs so she can enjoy what she has and be open to what may come. "People believe that you can have it all. I believe that you can, just not all at the same time. To me, having it all means being happy with who you are in life." Bridges clearly is, showing that she is a singular sensation designing a future that she will look back on with pride.

Being Single Is Just Another Option

With Technology Entrepreneur JC Lamkin

I've often heard people say that necessity is the mother of invention, and that was certainly the case for Josie Cheri Lamkin. JC, as she likes to be called, is founder of Gypsy Lane Technologies, a graphic design technology and computer training company—a business she created so that she could work from home. She wanted to be able to look after her father, who was in his eighties, and her mother, who was in her seventies.

The University of Pennsylvania graduate is part of a growing demographic; in the United States one out of every five people is caring for aging parents. Of those surveyed in a 2007 CBS poll, 21 percent said they were presently or had been the caretaker of a parent in the past.[1] The data also revealed daughters were two times more likely than sons to be caring for a parent.

The youngest of five children, the responsibility fell on Lamkin to care for her parents, not only because of her age but also because of her marital status. It's a job Lamkin says she was groomed to assume since she was a young girl. "As I was growing up, it was sort of unspoken that that was what the youngest would do. I think it was a natural progression."

So when the time arose for Lamkin to actually care for her parents, she wasn't bitter about the situation; she embraced her role as caregiver. "I never had the chance to think about whether it was a burden or not. It just seemed natural." Still, Lamkin quickly had to revamp her thinking to find a way to balance having a career with making sure her family's needs were being met. She found it by using the opportunity as positive motivation for her to start her business, allowing her to chart a future that would give her financial security and time flexibility.

She took about thirty thousand dollars from her savings to start Gypsy Lane Technologies out of an office in the basement of her home. She began with just a few computers and some filing cabinets, and her business took off.

Lamkin is just the latest in a long line of African American women who choose to become entrepreneurs. According to the U.S. Census, "black women owned 547,341 companies in 2002, up 75 percent from five years before."[2] The Center for Women's Business Research says, "Businesses owned by women of color represented nearly one-third of all of the firms owned by persons of color." They projected that "based on recent growth rates, in 2002, there will be 14,116 minority women owned firms with revenues of $1 million or more, and 111 with 100 more employees."[3]

As if owning a successful business weren't enough, in 2006 Lamkin began discussing changes in the business world and advances in computer technology on her radio show, *Technically Speaking*, which airs on WNWR 1540 AM. Serving as both executive producer and host, Lamkin has made a name for herself as a technical genius.

Her busy schedule, which now also includes a partnership at the Center for Progressive Leadership and board memberships at the African American United Fund, the Philadelphia Congress of the National Congress of Black Women, and the Liberation Fellowship CDC, leaves little time for a serious relationship.

"Most of the women who are successful and have businesses that I know of—a lot of them make room for a family," she says. Lamkin finds that trying to juggle a relationship and a personal life is a temperamental process that she shies away from. She thinks there are always certain roles you have to fill as the other half in a couple, like being available to listen, support, and help your partner. She says, "At the same time, I do those things at the risk of losing a part of myself. So, in my experience being in a relationship, especially during the holidays, you wear yourself out, and it's not that much fun."

She says a significant other can be draining because a relationship doesn't provide for very much down time. "I want to relax when I do come home, and in a relationship you don't have the chance to relax. You have a responsibility to the other half to listen to how their day went, how it didn't go, and help them through it."

Although she is still unsure if marriage is in her future, Lamkin says she is learning to develop the traits necessary to maintain a long-lasting connection with another person. "I think it's more than possible. It's probably more likely now that I'm past thirty-five because I know myself a lot better, and I know people a lot better. I am able to be a lot more useful in a relationship." More specifically, she's learned to be understanding of men and what they expect from a mate. "I am learning more tolerance and patience with other people. That is, I understand that some men think of it as sort of a slap in the face to see a woman, especially a woman of color, who is focused on a career—on developing herself as a whole person and not seeing a relationship as a priority." Lamkin says any man who could possibly be a suitable mate for her would have to understand that she has no intention of abandoning her career for anyone.

Lamkin would rather take her professional highs over the ups and downs of a roller-coaster-like relationship. And should that mean she ends up without a husband, she's OK with that. She has no regrets about her life, including the possibility that she could miss out on mother-hood. "I have about fourteen nieces and nephews. I was an aunt by the age of two, so to me there is nothing new," she explains. She does not feel compelled to be a parent, at least not now.

Lamkin also says she doesn't buy into the theory that someone else is going to rescue you, as in a fairy tale. "I never had that dream. I always thought people who had that dream were suckers, really, 'cause when I look at marriage, from what I've seen, the woman gets really a raw deal or the short end of the stick." She says it's often the woman who forgoes her dream for the family chores, never living up to her potential. "Histor-ically, the woman is the one who cleans up, makes sure the household is the way it's supposed to be, cooks, and has the children and does the drudgery while the man goes out and does what looks to me to be fun. He goes out to do business, meet with clients, plan strategies," Lamkin says. To her, the challenge of being able to use all her intellect to make her own money, see her ideas come to fruition, and build a business that changes the lives of others is what makes her happy; it's a part of life she thinks she would've missed out on if she opted to get married.

She is checking things off her to-do list at a steady rate, something she thinks many women don't do because they feel pressured to meet the expectations of others. "Most people don't go along in life at their own pace. They think they are supposed to go to school, graduate, have a career, get married, and have kids and then die." She's certainly not planning to leave the earth without making sure that she enjoys her life and spends time improving the community and relaxing. "I hope that in five, ten years, I don't wake up and say to myself, 'You were really selfish. You could've tried to settle down.' But right now I don't have a timeline. I just see my career getting better, the business getting bigger, and that's about it." She is truly living up to her own expectations so far.

In a 2003 *Newsweek* article, author Ellis Cose met with a group of black women like Lamkin, whom he dubbed the "black, beautiful, accomplished but can't find a mate club." As part of his conclusion, Cose presumes two possible futures for these women. In the bleak vision, he predicts that African American women will increasingly lead lives filled with success but isolation. His slightly more optimistic view suggests that black women are simply going through a transitional period from which they will emerge and will find a way to balance happiness and success.[4] Lamkin believes she is the latter; a woman who has found her own sense of purpose and joy, even though she chooses not to marry. It's something she's done by following her dreams and rebuffing peer pressure that called for her to sacrifice her goals so she could marry a man.

By refusing to limit herself, Lamkin has found her happiness and the possibility of a future that is limitless. She contends that it's the kind of perspective everyone should have, even if that means bucking societal norms. "A lot of times women don't realize that they have options," she states. "It's not just chocolate and vanilla." To Lamkin, single is just another flavor to be sampled, one that allows her to quench her cravings as a businesswoman, a broadcaster, and a daughter now able to check on her parents whenever she needs or wants to.

Part Five

Over Thirty-five but Not Ready to Settle

If there is a magic number for women, thirty-five is it. It marks the age when the odds of getting married plummets below half. It is also when the likelihood of getting pregnant naturally decreases, while the probability of having a child with a birth defect increases. More important, turning thirty-five marks a kind of "middle age" for most women, a point that can send them desperately scurrying online and into bars and clubs to find anyone with whom they can settle down.

Webster's defines the word "settle" as "to become quiet or orderly" or "to take up an ordered or stable life," which perpetuates the notion that single women somehow live scattered and raucous lives. That negative perception is held not only by men; females also frequently see their lives as hopelessly out of control if they don't have a man or significant other.

Yet there are some women who resist this idea. While they never fathomed that they would be single over the age of thirty-five, they embrace the positive aspects of it. They use the freedom that comes along with singlehood to pursue the careers that eluded them earlier in life, to further their philanthropic aspirations, or to explore the world. For these ladies, swapping the single life for just any mate is not an option they are willing to consider at any age.

13

Captain in a Solo Army

With Army Captain Gwyneth Bradshaw

When one thinks of an army captain, a woman in her late thirties with no husband, no kids, and two master's degrees doesn't immediately spring to mind. But that description fits Gwyneth Bradshaw.

Bradshaw knew she was limiting her relationship possibilities when she selected this path. "For me, my active military duty career started late; it just began two years ago. Even then, people told me, 'Don't do that.' They said, 'Think. How are you going to get married? You're going to be traveling, and no man is going to want to deal with that.'" Bradshaw says she paused for a moment but went ahead with her plan. "I almost considered not going on active duty. I thought, 'You know, I am thirty-five, and I am trying to get married, so how am I going to find man who's going to deal with that type of lifestyle? . . . I'm an older captain. A lot of men around my age in the military are already married.'"

But Bradshaw quickly shook those thoughts off in lieu of a promising and desirable career as an army social worker. It's a decision she does not regret. According to a study published in the June 2008 *American Sociological Review,* she's not alone. The survey, which was based on data from the Pentagon's Survey of Active Duty Personnel, found that black and Latino servicemen and -women have a higher job satisfaction rate than their white counterparts. The author of the report, Jennifer Hickes Lundquist of the University of Massachusetts Amherst, says, "What's striking is that minorities express more satisfaction in military jobs than they do in civilian jobs." She says the reason is the structure of the military and its overall diversity. Because the service has more social and economic equality than the civilian job market, minorities and women often find or perceive their path to advancement to be easier.[1]

For Bradshaw the traditional path of getting married young and having kids right away was discouraged by her family. "My mom got married young, and both my grandmothers got married young, at around twenty-one, and they were all against me getting married young. They were all like, 'Get your education first; men will always be there. You have to know how to be able to take care of yourself.'"

So she concentrated on school and put dating on the back burner. "When I was going to school, they [my grandparents] would ask me if I was dating anybody." If she answered no, they would respond, "Good. Get your education. . . . Get your education." She continues, "That's what they'd say all through college. When they realized I was getting my master's degree, they were like 'Good. Get your education. Get a good job. Get a good place to live.'"

Bradshaw says her family's attitude abruptly changed soon thereafter. "When I got all that, they started saying, 'When are you going to settle down and get married?' Once I accomplished what they thought I should have to be successful, then they started putting pressure on me to get married."

The greatest stress came from her father. "My dad is the one who was really upset about it. At one point, when I thought I was going to marry this guy, I introduced him to my dad. His first comment was 'I was getting worried because I didn't think I was getting any grandchildren.'"

When that relationship ended, Bradshaw says she did a lot of soul searching. It took some time before she not only realized but believed that "just because I am not married doesn't make me a bad person." Bradshaw says before she was able to accept that, she'd made all the classic relationship mistakes. "I've gone through the half-a-man-is-better-than-no-man phase when I was in my twenties; that's done."

She says she also followed her heart and deferred her dreams to make a relationship work. It was a choice that left her feeling empty. "I actually dated someone in New York who, when he moved to Maryland, I followed him. I gave up everything to be with him, and as soon as I got there, it didn't work out. I told myself 'I will not make this mistake again.'"

Bradshaw says these missteps caused her to take stock. "I started concentrating on other things. I had a focal change. I used to say, 'I don't want to travel too much until I am married. I don't want to buy a house until I am married.' Then I got a financial planner, and he was like, 'Why are you waiting?' That's when I realized I was putting my life on hold for too many different things in life, and it wasn't happening. So, I was like, you know what, I am either going to waste time waiting for this person to come along, or I'm going to live and enjoy life as I go. I've been a lot happier since I changed my focal point."

She also realized that the idealistic picture of the husband, 2.5 kids, and a white picket fence wasn't the key to happiness. "I believe you can be married and still be lonely. I've seen people who have done it. I think that was also a factor for me to change."

And when her first grandfather passed away, she says, "My grandmother didn't know how to take care of herself, how to pay bills, how to fix things in the house or fix the car. I told myself when I heard her complaining—I think I was twenty-six—I said, 'I don't want to be like that. I don't want to be so dependent on a man or my husband that if I outlive him I can't function.'"

Bradshaw does think that her independent streak has scared off some men. "Men put their worth on material things or on what they can do for you; they have to be the provider. They are the ones who have to bring home everything. If you can do it yourself, some men do find it intimidating." So she's not surprised that sometimes when she tells a man about her educational achievements, it rattles him. "Because I have two master's degrees, I've even had guys tell me, 'What do you want with me? What can I contribute to you?' I've had other men ask me, 'You already have a house and this stuff, so what can I really do for you?'"

She says the answer to that question is that you can give yourself, but only if you are a secure guy who see her accomplishments and possessions as positive and nonthreatening. She wants the unique type of companionship you can't get from anyone else in your life. "You have your girlfriends for certain things, but there are some things they can't touch." Until she finds the right man, Bradshaw is happy being her own woman, coming and going as she pleases.

Her strong sense of individuality has caused her to bump heads with her romantic interests. "I've found a lot of guys try to control me. If they can't control the whole situation, they break things off with me, then come back to me later when they realize the mistake that they've made. Or they aren't ready for a commitment, and they expect a woman to wait several years. I'm not one of those women willing to do that either. I believe that men want to have their cake and eat it, too."

She is most agitated by the old double standard between the way driven men and ambitious women are viewed. "A female is looked at badly if she isn't married at a certain age. If it's a guy, then people say, 'He just hasn't found the right woman yet. He's just focused on his career and getting himself together.' For a female, it's always, 'She's focused too much on her career, and if she'd just slow down then maybe a guy would want to settle down with her.'" She says sexism explains why the genders are seen differently in society. Despite all of the advances women have made, the prevailing social view is still that women should put their careers on the back burner to become wives and mothers, especially as they get older.

Bradshaw says it has taken her a while to shrug off the negative comments she's heard about being an unmarried woman in her thirties. "You do get it a lot, where people do see my being over thirty-five and not married as a negative thing." She says that stems from old values that haven't kept pace with modern reality. "I think there are some things that we hold on to as tradition and expectations, so when it comes to people in this country getting married at a young age, that hasn't changed." She contends that it's time for the public's attitude to change. "It's about time that people realize that being thirty-five and not married doesn't mean that there is something wrong with you; it just means that the opportunity hasn't presented itself."

Of course, oftentimes the lack of a husband goes hand in hand with the absence of children in a woman's life. That's the case for Bradshaw. "I would prefer to be married to have a family. I think it's a lot harder to be a single mom out here these days, but I don't look down on it. I've considered that if I'm not married by a certain age, I will try to adopt." Ultimately, she says, "I will be disappointed if I don't get married, but I will still live my life. I won't slip into a deep depression, and I won't feel like I am less than a woman." Instead she will continue to trumpet her dreams as the captain in her own one-woman army.

14

Solo Flyer
With TV Producer Catherine McKenzie

*C*reating *specials for the* number one local television station in the country in New York is a dream come true for TV producer Catherine McKenzie. It's also led her to rack up thousands of frequent-flyer miles per year traveling to her home state of Minnesota. "I grew up in the Midwest and went to college there. I have a picture on my bookshelf of myself with nine other girls—we tried to have breakfast together every Thursday when we were in college. . . . I am the only African American in the picture. I am also the only one not married and one of only two that do not have children. . . . I think all of us thought we would be married by thirty with kids and that they would all be playing together."

It sounds like a scene out of the *Sex and the City* movie, in which four girlfriends meet and discuss men, sex, and love in leisurely outings together. Much like the characters in the film, nearly every player in McKenzie's life has gotten the typical happy ending, while she has not. However, similar to the oversexed character Samantha Jones, who is the only one in the film to end up unmarried, it's clear that McKenzie is likewise not displeased with the outcome of her life.

In New York, single women are everywhere. According to the 2005 U.S. Census American Community Survey, there were 770,000 more unmarried women than men in the New York City metro area, making it the nation's third-largest city for singles. Minneapolis, where McKenzie was raised, was ranked number two on a 2008 list of ten cities where the number of single men and women are nearly equal.[1] So it's not hard to see why McKenzie's family didn't anticipate her "perpetual" singlehood. "I think my family expected me to be married by now and have a few children—I think my friends did, too."

But on the East Coast, she finds that those she encounters, especially other people of color, don't have that traditional expectation. "I don't know if it's still *that* important anymore—especially in the African American community—because I know so many single African American women." McKenzie says the black females she's met living in the city accentuate independence in their lives rather than dwelling on their relationship status, an attitude she believes was adopted to rebel against the overwhelming pressure placed on these women by the rest of the African American community.

Growing up in the Twin Cities region, McKenzie wasn't surrounded by many black people. "When I was in high school, in a city that was 90 percent white, I used to think the black boys didn't date me because they thought it was better to date a white girl—or because their daddies were told they couldn't date white girls, and now it was OK, so they wanted to try it out." Her dating life didn't change much when McKenzie was in college back in the early nineties, either. "When I was in college, I really didn't care—I dated who I liked no matter what the color." In fact, at her alma mater, St. Olaf's College, there are currently only forty-one African American students out of an enrollment of around three thousand.

She says that shortly after college she gave up worrying about finding a date; it's a situation she says many African American women find themselves in. "I think for so many black women, they are tired of fighting to get a date so they just stop trying. It feels like we fight each other, white women, society, every day just to get to work and go to the grocery store. And then you have to fight to get a date, too?" McKenzie continues by saying that the frustration over having to struggle to overcome so many obstacles in life leaves African American women with very little energy to vie for the attention of a man. She believes that at one point or another, "A lot of us stopped putting ourselves out there because we think there's no chance, so why bother." She says the defeatist attitude quickly passes, however, because neither she, nor most other women she knows, want to be single forever. She thinks there are suitable mates available, it just takes a lot of effort to find one. "I don't buy all the stats that there aren't enough men out there. I just think we have to be more creative with how and where we look for them."

McKenzie says that statistics on how black women are increasingly having trouble finding and meeting men actually gave her inspiration to turn her attention elsewhere. "First, it was a sign that I am not alone. Those numbers in a way gave me freedom; freedom *not* to worry about not being married. It let me concentrate on things that I really enjoy instead of worrying about not having a date."

What she focused on was developing her career in television production, which eventually took her from Minnesota to the Big Apple. "Because I'm a journalist, there was a point in my life when I lived in five cities in four years—those were years when a lot of my friends were meeting the 'loves of their lives' and getting married. . . . I was just trying to remember what my zip code was and how to get to work."

Her work has garnered a Peabody Award for ABC news coverage of the September 11 attacks as well as an award for her series *Love, Marriage, and Money.* She's also become renowned as a show producer with a keen ability to spot talent, having booked the Black Eyed Peas and Josh Kelly on *Eyewitness News Weekend* before they made it big.

In addition to getting accolades, McKenzie assumed a position as vice president of broadcasting for the New York Association of Black Journalists. The organization is responsible for providing more than fifty-five thousand dollars in scholarship funds in an effort to cultivate minority talent. It also provides an annual eight-week workshop for high school students that have an interest in the journalism industry. Besides her job, McKenzie says she also decided to "concentrate on my friendships with both men and women, making them quality relationships." Part of that process was stepping up to raise money when one of her closest friends, Elissa (E.J.) Levy, was diagnosed with multiple sclerosis at the age of thirty-three. McKenzie has been credited with bringing in more than three hundred thousand dollars to fund research for a cure for MS. She is also now a board member on Levy's charity, MS Hope for a Cure.

Being there when the chips are down isn't the only way that McKenzie shows her support for her friends. Helping them to achieve their own dreams is also at the top of her agenda. McKenzie assumed a role on the board of the Gotham Stage Company, which brings previously unproduced works by emerging artists to life in New York City. Her ability to devote time to significant causes is a positive side of being unattached and having no children.

In the midst of some of her greatest triumphs came her most crushing loss to date, the death of her father. It was during his illness and ultimate death that she realized the unique challenges of being single and being an only child. "Having already cared for one sick parent by myself, I think when my mother dies I will really feel alone."

McKenzie's isn't unique in her situation: caregiving for elderly parents is often an only child's responsibility. Author Karen Cook writes that even as youngsters, kids with no siblings are aware that it will be their job to take care of their parents as they get older. Cook says there is an upside to the predicament. Only children don't ever have to argue with anyone over their choices or have someone second guess the care they provide.[2] The drawbacks, however, are exactly what McKenzie fears: going it alone, with no financial or emotional support, no one to relieve her.

It is the assistance of a fallback person that McKenzie envies. "I remember being at my grandmother's funeral in my twenties and seeing my mother with her two siblings at the altar, really realizing that I would never have that kind of community. I would have to make those types of connections on my own."

She says that for now her friends are her family, but she would like someone special in her world who could truly be a support to her. "Being an only child, I don't want to grow old by myself. I want to be able to share that with someone." But she's quick to point out that it's not because she's ungrateful for the relationships she has in her life. "It's more of a matter of wanting to share the blessings in my life with someone than it is wanting to have someone there just to have someone there." McKenzie also says that after long hours at work, the reassurance of a significant other would be welcomed. "I do not consider myself lonely, but I do feel alone sometimes. There are times, especially after a long day at work, where all I really want to do is come home and cuddle on the couch with someone."

She believes that even secure people, or those at peace with being single, feel the need to have someone else around at certain times. "I believe that we are meant to share our thoughts and feelings with other human beings, and sometimes making a phone call or meeting someone out for a drink just isn't the connection that I am looking for. Sometimes I want to come home and chill with someone—although I do love my time on my couch alone." She says this internal conflict between wanting togetherness and enjoying solitude is easy to resolve if you find the right partner. But if she doesn't find that man, she says, "I would rather be single than be in a bad relationship."

However, realizing that time continues to pass and her desire to be a mother isn't waning, she has started to think about her options of becoming a parent. She says, "I have just started to think along these lines." McKenzie continues, "I really feel that, for me, a child needs two parents." But, she continues, "on the other hand, I also feel like I have a lot to give a child." Coming across stories and information about parentless children is shifting her thinking. "I get so upset when I see so many minority children in foster care that I feel I should adopt one—but I'm not sure yet that I could really do it well on my own." That uncertainty has kept her from acting on her maternal yearning, but she's unsure for how long.

She hopes that by the time she can no longer ignore her desire for motherhood there will be someone by her side. But he has to be the right someone. "He does have to have the same emotional maturity as me. He has to be able to support me, which means telling me when I'm wrong, as well as telling me when I'm right."

McKenzie isn't putting pressure on herself to tie the knot, but she has come to understand why there is so much emphasis on it from society. "I suppose there are some that think that it's a sign of passage—that it connotes a certain sense of emotional maturity—but these days, with so many couples getting divorced, I think it's more emotionally mature when you are *not* getting married. It shows that you are waiting to get married for the right reasons."

Until the right reasons are revealed to her, she will continue to rack up frequent flyer miles, happily caring for her mother in Minnesota, traveling the world for her television jobs, and making sure she is wherever her friends need her to be.

15

Rewriting the Rules of Single Life

With Technical Writer Lacy Lewis

"*I don't hope to marry* or not to marry. What I hope and pray is that I am the best person that I can be in every situation, and if marriage is on the table at some point, then I hope to be able to approach it from the right mindset and have the wisdom to do it for the right reasons," says Lacy Lewis. Being able to distinguish between getting married because it is what society expects as opposed to it being the correct choice for you is an attitude she believes all women should aspire to have. It's a way of thinking that empowers women to be active participants in their destiny rather than just passively accepting who and whatever comes their way.

Lewis is a technical writer, a professional who designs, creates, maintains, and updates technical documentation for Siemens Energy and Automation. She's built her career giving instructions to others on how to operate sophisticated equipment, but she says there is nothing more complex than navigating human relationships. Lewis says, "On the surface for me, a career does not get in the way of my relationships. It can infringe at times, but if two people want to be married, they will work it out. Like Michelle and Barack Obama." She points out that anyone with a high-pressure job like hers just has to realize that "a career and a marriage are two different things. One is a priority and the other one is secondary. At times these may flip [in importance], but if it is agreed upon and understood that the flip is for the greater good, then it can be worked through. Having said that, I can admit there were days when I worked late into the evening and thought to myself, 'If I were married I could not do this.'"

But Lewis would not consider trading the life she has for the one she dreamed of as a child. "As a young girl I did not expect to be single at this age. I had expectations about marriage similar to everyone else," she says. She played dress up and envisioned her big day, which she imagined would be similar to something in a child's fairy tale. "I tried on my mom's wedding dress and dreamed of a love-at-first-sight, being-swept-off-my-feet type of affair. I imagined the two children and a house with a white picket fence. As a teenage girl I thought as most young girls do, and summed up every boy in terms of marriage material." The only exception was "that I would be a married professional in the business world, and my husband and I would be on equal footing. We would both become wealthy and then travel the world saving children and building orphanages internationally. This is what I imagined for as long as I can remember." She says she continued to do that even into her college years. At the time, she felt that "the man had special super powers that would save you from the world."

Her idealized life sounds similar to the tale of Lois Lane and Superman. By day Clark Kent is an average working guy toiling beside his dutiful partner; at night he dons a cape and protects her and others from the evil villains in the world, even circumnavigating the globe to reverse the wrongs that have been done to her. Unfortunately that's not reality. Men don't have superpowers, and they can't save women from the bad things that may come their way. All they can do is love them.

Lewis is no longer holding out for a knight in shining armor, but she says she doesn't agree with the expectation that just because she's in her forties she's aged out of the marriage category. "I do believe that you can get married at forty, fifty, or sixty . . . and be just as happy as if you were married at twenty or thirty." She's correct. *Newsweek* magazine did a follow-up on its infamous 1986 article that predicted "women after 30 had a 20 percent chance of getting married. For women over 40, those chances plummeted to 2.6 percent." New research shows that the twenty-year-old numbers were inaccurate because they failed to take into account the cultural changes that took place, such as women working, getting more degrees, and becoming financially independent. Instead the statistics reflected a time when women where getting married by age twenty. The reality is that the marriage probability for women over forty is much better than previously thought. It appears that the odds of a woman getting married over the age of forty are at least 40 percent or greater.[1]

Women who are more mature know what they can and cannot deal with in a relationship. "When I was younger it was adventurous to struggle with your man and build your world around him, but when you get into your forties, you should really be dealing with someone who is already established." Lewis says emphatically, "Believe me when I say that struggling at twenty is a lot different than struggling at forty." She now knows that "marriage is not a piece of paper of ownership or some ill-gotten gain. The idea of marriage is simply about the desire or willingness to share your love, life, positive energy, and, most important, space and time with another whole, well-developed, or well-healed human being." That's something she didn't get in her twenties, and that's what made the struggle to keep a relationship together all the more difficult.

She continues, "Marriage is a lot of work. You have to be ready for that type of commitment and confident and honest enough to know that you can withstand the demands of that type of relationship." Lewis is quite relieved she's not married at the present time because she says, "If I want to fly to the moon tomorrow, I can. It actually feels quite liberating. I love it! I don't know if, when I was younger, I would have thought being single at forty would feel so good, but it is like you have this wisdom, and then on top of that you have this freedom, too. It's really exhilarating."

She pauses and then points out, "I don't think anyone goes into this expecting not to be married; however, you should embrace where you are and love you at any place, as long as you can find the joy in that place. If not, then you need to look deeper at yourself before you start looking at other options—like marriage—for the wrong reasons."

Lewis has done that kind of introspection, and says, "I have gotten to know me and love me and laugh with me in a way that only makes me smarter, wiser, funnier, and much more open to sharing myself as a confident, peace-filled champion of love who makes wiser choices in partnerships. I can't say I know everything I like, but I certainly know what I don't like."

She considers herself lucky "or very fortunate that I did not make a decision based on the wrong things and become miserable in the process. More important, I consider myself smart for not bringing children into an incomplete relationship. It's hard enough for children to figure out the world around them without having to try to figure out the world inside of their own home. I am not lonely, because I have family and friends and loved ones that keep me engaged in life. I date, I travel, and I am socially outgoing. I am not alone because well, from a spiritual perspective, I can never be alone. It is just what I believe."

Because of her perspective, she doesn't dwell on her single status. Instead, she says, "I don't think of it in terms of aging single; I think about it in terms of growing wiser and gracefully exploring life's options other than marriage." One of those options is traveling to exotic places throughout the world. "I have an extremely adventurous spirit. I want to explore and travel and learn more and more. And to be able to get up and go without asking permission is *awesome*!" She's not alone. According to www.gutsytraveler.com, about 32 million single American women traveled at least once in the last year.

While Lewis doesn't feel that she needs to married to be fulfilled, she says she understands why relationships are such a focal point in our society. "They are the most important threads, weaving their way through every fiber of the life of mankind, and marriage is believed by most of the world to be an experience second to none, including child-birth. And I believe wholeheartedly in it [marriage], if it is for the right reasons. If it is with the right person, if you are whole and complete and ready to give and receive. But I don't think it should ever be rushed or dependent upon your biological clock or a point to prove or a way to save your soul, sensibilities, or economics. It is a thread that you weave into many generations to come, and you need to be careful what materials you add to the fabric of your life."

If that right person does not come along, adding a child to her life is still something she says she may consider. But she does not want to give birth as a single mother. "A child will ask at some point, 'Who and where is my father?' I don't want to be that mother if I don't have to be. So no, for the sake of the child I would not pursue having children alone. I would, however, consider adoption."

Lewis says that while she's not overwhelmed by the urge to be married and have children, it is clear why many people are. "I guess it is a natural part of our existence to want to unite with a partner, to procreate. I don't think anything is wrong with that, but I don't understand when the need supersedes the common sensibilities or basic intellect—then there is a problem. Women, to me, want men for so many reasons other than love. They need them to replace their fathers, to feel wanted, to get away from home to prove a point to their parents or friends, for confirmation of self, etc. . . . I could go on and on."

She says a growing legion of women like herself are finally reaching for self-joy rather than seeking out marriage as a means to fill the voids in their lives. "I think it is not just black women; I think it is generational and an American phenomenon. Women work and make huge salaries in America, making them less dependent on marriage. Although women may desire it at some level, it is no longer the priority, and that is because there are so many other directions to go in terms of priority."

What makes the phenomenon unique for black women is that they have generations of women to draw from. "Black women in my experience have had an opportunity to look at the past generations in their families where, for many, the mother has struggled to keep the family together, sometimes with the father's help and sometimes without it, even though the father may have been in the picture." She says that fueled our ancestors to raise their daughters with a drive to be self-sufficient, not antimale as is often thought. "I think many black women have heard their mothers tell them, 'Get your education; you don't need a man to do this. Wait to get married. There is no rush to jump into this and have a bunch of children.' We have been told, 'Don't put yourself in a situation you can't walk away from. Have your education and career first and then a family.' It is a combination of the women's liberation movement and the move away from the shackles of slavery, influenced by misogynistic relationships that formed out of desperation and need more than desire, that pushes many mothers and grandmothers to direct their daughters away from marriage and toward a happily single existence."

Lewis is reflective about her own life experiences that show this. She says, "My mother and father and maternal grandmother were very influential in my life, and they all constantly told me I would have to make it on my own first so that I never have to depend on a man or anyone else to sustain me. They impressed upon me how important it was for me and my mate to be in the relationship for the right reasons (i.e., love, friendship, companionship, good conversation, and similar interests and education)."

In light of this fact, she scoffs at the data that indicates that black women are increasingly single, saying it's far more important for a woman to know that there is an option to be single if she doesn't find someone who shares the essentials needed for a healthy, happy union. "There will always be some *odd* statistic that is not very complimentary to black women. It does bother me that black women seem to be a part of some of the worst statistics, and if you don't have a good dose of self-esteem, you could be overwhelmed and buy into a lot of these so-called statistics. Statistics for me don't apply. I have one supplier and from a spiritual perspective that is the only one that can determine my odds in life."

One major thing that she's done to change the likelihood of her finding a mate is that she no longer feels confined to dating just black men. "The world is like an oyster, why not experience it all? I have not dated within the Caucasian race, but I no longer dismiss the idea—not because I am older and feel my options are limited but just because I am wiser and understand the landscape of relationships better and real-ize that color plays a much smaller part than even I had thought. Every woman should travel the world. For me it breaks down to culture more than color."

But Lewis adds that "I don't need a man. I feel very confirmed in my skin. Thank God. Don't know why, but that is just the way it is for me; however, I do desire great friendships, partnerships, love, and joy, and if those come in the form of a man, then that is great. But that is my desire, not my need."

Her advice for other single women struggling to find their place in a conventional world is not to get down on themselves or let anyone or anything keep them from rewriting the rules of single life until they define their happiness. She says, "All the good people of the world keep moving and shaking regardless of 'singledom'!"

Part Six

Divinely Single

Seeing single life as a blessing rather than a curse may be foreign to some women, but for those with a strong sense of faith it makes perfect sense. If you're wondering why, the answer may be because to the devoted everything in life happens according to God's plan, including when and if they find their mate.

Americans are overwhelmingly spiritual. According to a www.ABCNews.com poll, 83 percent of those surveyed identify themselves as Christians. In the African American community, religion has always played a huge role, dating as far back as slavery times; that tradition continues today.

Recognizing that such a large portion of the population embraces faith is crucial to understanding how marriage and family are viewed within society. Religion is often used to establish the guidelines for what one looks for in a mate and in a relationship. According to a 2007 study from the Pew Research Center entitled "Trends in Attitudes Toward Religion and Social Issues," about 76 percent of Americans say that their faith is the basis for maintaining a traditional outlook on family and marriage. However, this marks a decline of about 9 percent over a decade ago, meaning attitudes are starting to become more liberal.

Still, for those who hold religious doctrine close to their hearts, the tools and ideas they need to navigate life have been given to them in their chosen dogma. Faith provides them with comfort when they are lonely, peace when they are afraid, and the reassurance that, if they live as instructed, all that they need will be provided.

For single women, faith provides the hope that if they are meant to share themselves with someone, that person will be placed in their path. If not, they will remain single, but divinely so—filled with the knowledge that there is another plan for their life, and that's just fine with them.

16

Single According to God's Plan

With Business Owner Camille Young

"*I am single but not alone,*" declares Camille Young, the owner of BaGua Juice Bar in Jersey City. "I have many friends, I have my business, and I have God." It is her faith in a higher power that comforts Young and provides her with the solace that she isn't ever truly alone.

Young says her beliefs explain why she isn't attached. "I feel I am not married because it is not time. Yes, I do believe that my choices govern my life, and focusing on my business does not leave much time for meeting eligible bachelors. But I also believe that God makes a way out of no way when it is in His plan. So if meeting a great guy and getting married is in His plan, it will happen in spite of me and my focus."

Young has faith that the words in Ecclesiastes 3, 1–8 are true for her life:

There is a time for everything,
And a season for every activity under heaven

Young doesn't question God's timing or the possibility that she will be shown her "Adam." Rather her focal point is on franchising her business and making sure she doesn't have to return to corporate America, which she found depressing. Young says, "Seeing how many people who looked like me were treated was smothering. My creativity needed freedom, so I left to run my own business."

The successful thirty-something entrepreneur's business is thriving, but her dating life has not blossomed yet—which makes her fall short of the societal expectation that she be wed by now. "I'm sure my mom thought I would be married with at least one grandchild for her by now. I am an only child, so I know she really wants this . . . but she never placed pressure on me." Young says that lack of stress has allowed her to relax when it comes to dating until she finds "the one."

"I would like to find that special person for me . . . that person who will appreciate me and who I can appreciate. That person that just feels right. If that leads to marriage, great; if not, I would be grateful for the connection in general." So far, though, "There is not a question in my mind now that I was not supposed to marry any one of the guys I dated. They were not right for me."

The prevailing thought that there is someone who is a good fit for each of us is something Young says is implanted from the time we are small. She says, "We were taught by those who experienced the importance of it. This is just what they knew, and that is all that they could teach us. It is also a way at times for people to escape the reality of themselves [hence the rate of divorce, abuse, etc.] or to 'keep up with the Joneses.' All of my friends are married with children. If I were more of a follower, I would be married by now just because everyone else is."

But Young says she's always challenged standard notions on just about everything in her life. "Every aspect of my life rises above statistics." She says it's thought that being "an only child raised by a single mom who had me at eighteen would mean that I would have gotten pregnant at an early age based on statistics." Yet she is still childless in her thirties. She says she also "had no real educational direction, but I managed to be one of the top in my class at every school . . . This defies stats." Further, she says, attending "a top college, succeeding in the workforce, completing a master's, and owning a business for almost three years as a black woman, defies the law of averages."

She's willing to do one more nontraditional thing on her own: have a child. "In fact, I always said this, and maybe it is because my mom raised me just fine. I will, however, make sure that I am in a financial position to raise my child or children without 'lack' etched in their surroundings."

Any man who wants to join Young's life will have to be as driven to achieve as she is. "They have to be at a point in their lives that is self-sustaining. I will not take on a man's learning curve when it comes to business." She says, "The most important thing for me, though, is that they [the man] reach me in that way that I know they were meant for me. The rest is secondary."

She wants a love like the one described in the biblical passage, Song of Solomon 8:6:

Place me like a seal over your heart,
Like a seal on your arm,
For love is as strong as death,
Its jealousy unyielding as the grave.
It burns like blazing fire

Young thinks getting this unrestricted kind of love will be difficult for her because she is "very used to my space, and it will probably be a challenge for me to open it up. I've grown a little more guarded over the years as well, and that is something I want to work on. I am naturally a giver and a lover, and I don't want to lose those traits because of past relationships or the comforts of single life."

The peace she feels allows Young to have no regrets at all about being single. In fact, it has allowed her to be OK with who she is and not to tie her identity to her marital status. "I don't feel this [being single] is a trait to hold on to, to emulate or to honor, nor is it something to hide, regret, or be ashamed of. . . . It's just not something I focus on."

She says what is important for women to concentrate on is "to be true to themselves. To live their lives as they want, not as they see others living theirs. To always make sure that they treat themselves with honor, respect, and love and to demand this of anyone they bring into their lives."

Young points out that she is a "strong believer that there is someone out there who complements me, that we all have this. Being a heterosexual woman, I feel that someone is a man — but the right man, not just any man."

Until or unless that happens, she's determined to live her life as a woman not defined by the presence or absence of a gold band on her finger. "If it is in my destiny to get married, I will. If I don't, then it is not because I traded that path in." To Young, it will be because God had a different plan for her future, one that will allow her never to be lonely because she has His love.

17

Single and Refusing to Settle

With Nonprofit Chairperson Sidney Morris

In March 2008 the *Atlantic Monthly* published an article by Lori Gottlieb called "Marry Him." In it, the author concludes:

> [W]omen should "settle"! That's right. Don't worry about passion or intense connection. Don't nix a guy based on his annoying habit of yelling "Bravo!" in movie theaters. Overlook his halitosis or abysmal sense of aesthetics, because if you want to have the infrastructure in place to have a family, settling is the way to go.[1]

For Sidney Morris, that's not even an option. "I think the main reason I am not married is because I was not willing to settle." The forty-two-year-old has known women who opted for this route to the altar and has seen that it didn't pay off the way they thought. "I know many others who married for convenience, because they wanted a father for their children—being nothing more than children themselves—because it was what everyone else wanted them to do, or because they already accepted the proposal but didn't want to say they had a change of heart. I like my life as a single person and am not pushing the marriage card."

Gottlieb contends that Morris's friends made the right choice by marrying "Mr. Good Enough," a person who provides a stable, reliable life while serving as a companion.[2] But, Morris counters that too many women buy this argument, opting for miserable lives rather than learning to be happy with themselves. She says she's her own comfort and her own best friend, so finding a mate is not a requirement. "I was not one who sat and dwelled on being with someone, but rather took the approach that if it happened, it happened."

So far it hasn't happened for Morris, but she feels fine about that. She says, "I never really hoped for marriage." She did desire motherhood, though. "The only regret I have about being single is not having children. I would have loved to have had a son. . . . Being a forty-two-year-old woman, I believe that the time has come and gone." Morris has found a way to use those maternal instincts to shape the lives of young people, though. "I chair the board for the Weaver Foundation, Inc., which is a not-for-profit organization focused on reducing recidivism of female offenders. We are focused on providing life skills to female offenders and pairing them with transitional housing prior to their reentry into society."

Gottlieb argues that the biological clock is one major reason why women should settle: "Those of us who choose not to settle in hopes of finding a soul mate later, are almost like teenagers who believe they're invulnerable to dying in a drunk driving accident. We lose sight of our mortality. We forget that we, too, will age and become less alluring. And even if some men do find us engaging, and they are ready to have a family, they'll likely decide to marry someone younger with whom they can have their own biological children."[3] However, Morris finds that her friends and family have painted a mixed picture of motherhood; making her feel as if she hasn't missed out on anything at all in her life by not choosing to procreate with the wrong man just to have a child. "As for children, many have said I would make a good mother and would love

to see me with children. Others have said, 'Girl, count your blessings.' "
That's exactly what Morris chooses to do: count her blessings and opportunities she acted on rather than the things she's let pass by.

Morris says women, especially black women, have more choices
than they've ever had before. After decades of having to battle against sexism and racism in the workplace, African American women are no longer
relegated to menial labor and low-paying jobs; they are making strides in
corporate America that have heightened their sense of self-worth. "Black
women are strong, and as time goes by, more and more black women are
seeing that they have skills and abilities, and they are exploring them."
Morris continues, "Black women are more career minded in this century and are taking leaps of faith to establish their own. It doesn't mean
they can't do these things and be married; it just means more and more
black women are defeating the odds and refusing to settle." She states
that times have simply changed. "We are no longer living in the era of
being married by a certain age and being 'barefoot and pregnant.'"

She claims society is not being honest about the reality of the state
of marriage and the family. She says it's often held up as a panacea; that
if women enter this union they'll never be lonely, they'll have perfectly
well-adjusted children, and that they'll be financially secure. However,
the truth is that fewer people are getting married and those who do are
getting divorced at an astounding rate. "I am not sure that marital status
is still important in today's society, as is evidenced by the high divorce
rate, adultery that seems to be ever increasing, and the percentage of
single individuals in America." The fallout from bad, destructive, or
failed marriages may be more detrimental to women than never having
been married at all, because the scars left behind tend to hinder future
relationships.

Morris knows why some women feel it's imperative to have a man in
their life. "I believe there are some women who define success by being
married. Some give in to the odds that barriers cannot be broken for

single black women to be successful. Others feel the need to find fathers for their children. Some say they want to 'live right,' so in order to satisfy their sexual urges in a manner that is not against the word of God, they marry. Finally, many women are simply afraid of being alone."

Being alone isn't something that frightens Morris, and that's because she knows there's a huge difference between being physically alone and being lonely. "You know, I don't consider myself alone or lonely. That being said, that does not mean I don't think about being with someone or feel lonely at times. Being lonely is a state of mind." She goes on to say, "I know of married women who, whether married for one year or twenty-five years, are lonely. When I think of being lonely, I think of having no one around me and being in a depressing state; being isolated if you will." She certainly doesn't live an isolated life. She's constantly surrounded by friends, family, and church members. She's also filled her life with love from the women she tries to help stay out of prison.

And Morris is quick to point out that living alone does have its perks. She declares there's no "drama, at least, in my home. Oh, and one other important thing: aging as a single person probably adds more years to your life and you will probably have less gray hair."

On a serious note, Morris states, "Aging as a single woman provides the opportunity to tap into who you really are. You are able to do a great deal of soul searching to find out more about the inner you." She pauses, then continues, "Can you do this when you are married? Absolutely, but the search for self is often clouded by the overwhelming association of being someone's wife. You begin to define who you are in the marriage as opposed to who you are as an individual."

Morris would rather be defined by who she is as a person than by her marital status. She points out that at least she lives an authentic life, one that makes her truly happy and isn't affected by what others think about her. "So many married people are fakes and project this image of being a happy couple because they are so concerned about what other people think. When you really know the person you see that is not the case, but they would rather 'fake it to make it.'"

And marrying someone just to avoid being by herself or because data say if she doesn't settle she could end up alone isn't for her. "I would not enter into a marriage because statistics say I may not be able to make it as a single black woman; that is not the foundation on which marriage is built." She says her life, and the lives of other women like her, prove that it is possible to excel on your own.

But Morris also wouldn't rule out a potential spouse just based on arbitrary reasons. "I would not turn down someone of the same level of success, money, and power in the same way that I would not turn down a man who didn't have these things. The key is that we have a strong connection." However, she says just being in love with someone isn't a compelling enough reason for her to walk down the aisle either. "Many will say, 'As long as we love each other that is all that matters.' I don't agree with that. It takes a lot to make a relationship work, and I am sorry, but in today's world, that includes money. If he is a worker and has the mindset and ambition to progress, that works for me."

Morris points out that she's not "holding out" for anyone; she's just living her life with the knowledge that if God sends someone across her path she'll be ready. She says, "My faith has been an inspiration to me." She quotes the biblical passage Hebrews 11:1: "Faith is the substance of things hoped for and the evidence of things not seen." While she hasn't yet seen a man she wants to spend her life with, she believes that it is greater that she lives a "full and exciting life shared with many."

Her faith has taught her that "more than anything, it is OK to be single, and there is nothing wrong with that. I am fearfully and wonderfully made in the image of God, period!"

Part Seven

Musings on Single Life

As I ruminate about my own life as a single black woman, it occurs to me that some of the assumptions that have been made about the other women in the book have not been made or have easily been dismissed about me. I've been truly fortunate to be surrounded by a plethora of other single women and a host of married African American females, none of whom question the absence of a ring on my finger.

I must concede that the reason for that may be that, like a lot of women, for most of my adult life I have been involved in one long-term relationship or another. It has been my existence as a serial monogamist that insulated me from queries about my sexuality, about whether I am hostile toward men, or about my willingness to get married. I have also been blessed with parents who recognized the fullness of my life regardless of my marital status and who have made little or no mention of their desire for me to be coupled.

Additionally, witnessing my mother and father work to maintain their relationship for more than forty years was beneficial for two reasons. I got to grow up in a two-parent black family, and I was shown how difficult it can be to keep a marriage together, to preserve your individuality, and to raise children. I became acutely aware that a union between a man and a woman is anything but a fairy tale — it is a complex merger that requires both people to be clear about their feelings for each other and their objectives as a unit. Observing this sobered me up to the fact that, especially when I was younger, I was ill equipped to be married.

Still, as I have aged I yearned for a partnership with a man. While I haven't found it all that difficult to meet someone I care about, I've witnessed other female friends of mine struggle to find a mate. Solving the mystery as to why successful, attractive women have a hard time meeting someone isn't easy. Several things are at play. For some, it's because their demanding careers leave them limited time to go out and meet someone. For others, it is the supposition on the part of men that they have everything they need materially and don't need what a man could offer them. There is also the notion that powerful women have very little interest in marriage all together. Of course I and many other women know that these thoughts could not be further from the truth. Despite this, an increasing number of black women find themselves suddenly single without any prospects of marriage.

For me the solution to this has been to focus on myself, my goals, and surrounding myself with love from family and friends. While I do have a significant other in my life, I know that should we end the relationship I would be heartbroken, but I would not be alone. The void in my life would be filled with other relationships that sustain me. I would also take solace in the knowledge that being single is often a temporary state, one we will all find ourselves in, and one there is no sense in lamenting.

18

Alone, Not Lonely

I Know That I Will Never Disappoint Myself

Webster's defines the word "alone" as "separated from others or isolated." Yet the lives and attitudes of the women in this book clearly show that many black women take issue with the idea that simply because they aren't married their lives seen as empty and devoid of love and loved ones. All of these women make it crystal clear that they have scores of friends and belong to groups and churches; they simply don't have a husband.

Still, when a woman doesn't have a spouse many people assume she's lonely, which Webster's defines as "unhappy as a result of solitude." But once again, these women aren't miserable at all. They enjoy travel, careers, and recreation and have lives that many married people would envy rather than pity.

The freedom and financial security enjoyed by singles compels more and more African American women either to remain unattached until they find someone who meets their criteria or to venture through life on their own accord, happily and peacefully.

Professor Bella DePaulo theorizes that sexual freedom is another driving force behind this trend. In her book, *Singled Out*, she says, "Neither men nor women need a spouse to have sex without stigma or shame. Children born to single mothers now have the same legal rights as those born to married mothers," thereby reducing the need for women to have a wedding to reproduce.[1] Furthermore, the obligation of marrying because of children has also been lessened by advances in birth control and reproductive technology that allow us to "have sex without having children and children without having sex."[2] And the former stigma attached to single motherhood has been significantly lessened. In fact, it's been embraced in the black community and no longer subjects children without a father in the home, by and large, to demeaning terms such as "bastard" or "illegitimate."

Author Maryann Reid turned her attention to shedding light on the subject in the 2005 book *Marry Your Baby Daddy*, using the interviews she'd done with hundreds of unmarried couples with children. The issue concerned her so greatly that she took it upon herself to try to reverse the trend by connecting supporters and vendors with couples interested in uniting their families. In 2007, ten couples with children were married in an all-expenses-paid ceremony during the second annual celebration of "Marry Your Baby Daddy Day."

Even with efforts to unite families, the label "baby mama" has become too commonplace. *American Idol* winner Fantasia Barrino sang about it on her CD *Free Yourself*. When she was vying for the top prize in the contest, she drew fire from some media outlets just because she is a single parent. Later she was celebrated for what has now become an anthem to those who know her struggles:

> I see you get that support check in the mail.
> Ya open it and you're like, "What the hell?"
> You say, "This ain't even half of the day care."[3]

Fantasia's depiction of life for a single mother is painfully accurate. According to the 2001 U.S. Census data, single women raising families had the greatest overall poverty rates. Of the 6.8 million families maintained by women with no spouse and living below the poverty line, 1.8 million of them were African American.

Still, the high rate of infidelity outweighs the financial benefit to women, making them reluctant to bind their lives to a man who might violate their trust. According to infidelity stats from Menstuff.org, 24 percent of men and 14 percent of women admit to being unfaithful during their marriages.[4] It also states that 17 percent of divorces in the United States are the result of cheating. However, it is unclear how accurate these numbers are, since they rely on the guilty party admitting indiscretion.

In the last decade, the independence of black women has been lauded by top R & B singers including Whitney Houston, whose hit "It's Not Right, but It's Okay" was the anthem to women dealing with a cheater. It points out how selecting to remain single is a better option than taking poor treatment from a man:

> Pack your bags, up and leave
> Don't you dare come running back to me.'
> . . .
> Close the door behind you leave your key
> I'd rather be alone than unhappy . . .[5]

Contemporary music has embraced the notion that it is better to be alone than to be mistreated within a relationship. In the last decade, scores of singers have sung tunes touting female independence. Grammy Award winning songstress Beyoncé is among them, belting out a string of profemale tunes, including "Me, Myself, and I," which encourages a woman to rely on herself for strength, friendship, and comfort rather than a man who will leave or betray her.

> Me myself and I
> That's all I got in the end
> . . .

I take a vow that from now on
I'm gonna be my own best friend . . .[6]

Singer Tamia's song "Me" skyrocketed up the charts. Its focus was an inspirational tale of a woman leaving a man who didn't provide her with the love she needs. She finds that she has the strength within herself to be alone without being unloved. The chorus is:

And her name is me,
And she loves me more than you'll ever know
And I finally see that loving you and loving me
Just don't seem to work at all[7]

However, even in the world of popular music, the common notion remains that a woman should have a man by her side. In fact, songs frequently dramatize the dire consequences a woman faces if she is single by choice or circumstance. That's certainly the case in the song, "No Air" by *American Idol* winner Jordin Sparks. The lyrics to this tune describe a woman who is unable survive on her own when her significant other leaves:

Tell me how I'm supposed to breathe with no air
Can't live, can't breathe with no air
That's how I feel whenever you ain't there
there's no air, no air[8]

The desperation depicted in this song and many others shows how the female psyche is bombarded with subliminal as well as blatant messages that singlehood is equivalent to a slow death. Thus it's easy to understand why some women feel torn between remaining single and perpetually having a man on their arm, even a "piece" of a man, else risk ruin and despair.

Worse than that, black women who thicken their skin and choose to move forward by excelling in their career without worrying about finding a man are often thought to be bitter or angry. Many dispel this expectation but honestly admit that while they are not hostile, they are frustrated by the ease with which they've been able to forge forward professionally but not personally.

Despite this, African American women keep their chins up and strive to blaze trails in the arenas commonly dominated by the men. They forge ahead in the boardroom and in personal endeavors such as home ownership, entrepreneurship, and parenthood with the love and support of family and friends. Although they haven't given up on finding a male partner, they are clear that they only want one if he meets their terms.

The strong family and social ties enjoyed by the black women in this book and elsewhere serve as an example for all women that romantic love is not the only fulfilling kind of love. Being enveloped by others who serve as a support system frequently replaces the need for—or even occupies the space of—a man. When these single women are sick, bored, or just in need of someone to pass the time, their empathetic, compassionate, and devoted significant others of all genders provide them with an emotional outlet, a social life, and sometimes just distraction, and the result is that they never feel as if they are missing out on anything. For many, spending time with their girlfriends and family is the interaction that they desire, so the absence of a man is noticed, possibly even felt, but it doesn't limit their happiness or result in their being lonely.

19

Suddenly Single

The Social Pressures on Single Sistahs

Answering the question of why black women increasingly find themselves suddenly single for decades longer than ever before isn't simple. For every woman, the "why" is different.

The expectations arc that African American women want a man who has the same income, if not more, than she has; that a career-oriented or highly successful woman doesn't have or doesn't make time for a relationship; that every woman wants to be rescued; that black women who have been single for a long time are irrationally angry all the time and therefore impossible to get along with.

There is also the notion that every woman yearns to marry and have children because her biological clock is ticking. And if a woman is single and sexually active, she's a tramp or a whore without any standards for whom she lays down with. If a woman happens to have a child out of wedlock, she's not datable because she must be embroiled in baby daddy drama.

If a woman has been married before, the prevailing thoughts as to why she doesn't have a man now are that she drove off her husband with unreasonable demands, that she's bitter or angry because she's divorced, or, if she has children, that she's just looking for a father for them.

Certainly women like Kim Coles, Sheila Bridges, Deborah Gregory, and countless others clearly prove that these beliefs aren't true. So what does account for the growing number of unmarried black women?

Many women say their own lack of interest, the unwillingness of men to pop the question, and their lack of self-knowledge are partly responsible. Whatever the cause, an enormous number of African American women feel it's less important to focus on the marriage they don't have than the close relationships with friends and family they do have. It is the deep self-awareness that they've gained from looking inward that's given them the key to happiness and peace, allowing them to come to terms with a life without a husband and, in some cases, children.

But it's clear that an abundance of black women have gained this tranquility only after struggling against social messages and pressures that condemn, ridicule, and often trivialize their lives as single women. One example of this message comes from the show *The Bachelor*, which features desperate women vying for a proposal from a man they've known less time than their car mechanic. And this show provide a tame image of what lengths women in general will and do go through to get a man.

The VH1 hit series *The Flavor of Love* was a grotesque display of female desperation. In the program, scantily clad, mostly black women compete for the attention of rehabilitated drug addict, baby daddy, and questionably attractive rap pioneer Flavor Flav. These ladies, and I use the term loosely, allow him to kiss and grope them at whim, all for the alleged chance at "love." Of course, as several seasons went by, it became clear that true partnership was not what Flavor Flav was truly after; he was there for the temporary companionship and fame. The most disturbing thing about the show was the low standards these women were willing to accept under the pretext of getting the man. They cut each other down, dressed skimpily, dumbed themselves down, and shared pieces of one man. I wish the show were an anomaly, but I suspect its overwhelming popularity struck a common, all-too-familiar nerve with both men and women. The good news is that this show has finally seen its last taping, so it can only be hoped that the impressions it may have given about black women fades as quickly as its contract with the network did. Still, its mere existence hurt the overall image of women and their perception of themselves by providing them with the message that in order to get the attention of a man—thereby achieving their fairy-tale ending—they have to behave in a demeaning manor.

Television isn't the only medium that paints a dismal picture of life as an unmarried black woman. The idea that no matter what they accomplish as independent women, their existence is unfulfilling if there is no man by their side remains popular in the movie industry, too. In *How Stella Got Her Groove Back*, the female leads loses her job at a financial company then retreats to Jamaica with her girlfriend only find a younger man who inspires her to rebuild her life. Queen Latifah starred in a movie called *Last Holiday*, in which she is mistakenly diagnosed with a fatal disease. After evaluating her life, which is filled with fantasies about getting married, she travels overseas to try new things before her life is over. Of course her dream man arrives on the eve of her learning she will live, and the two of them live happily ever after. Still no movie is more infamous than *Waiting to Exhale* for its depiction of women as pathetic creatures whose lives revolve around and are destroyed by the whims of men. The 1999 motion picture based on the Terry McMillan novel follows four successful women living and working in Phoenix, Arizona. The girlfriends have very little in common, except for their poor choice in men. Here's a character breakdown:

Savannah Jackson, played by singer Whitney Houston, is a successful television producer who is in love and sleeping with a married man. She falls into the clichéd trap of a woman thinking that a man is going to leave his wife for her. She is a classic example of how bright, talented women are often shown as weak, ruled by their heart and not their head; their libido rather than their morals.

She's not to be outdone by the Robin Stokes character, who is not only having an affair with a married man, but will also sleep with any man. She's the classic single woman who is sexually promiscuous.

Bernadine Harris is a brilliant, highly educated woman who passed up her dreams to build a life and business with her husband only to later be left for a white woman. This passé story line is not only misleading, it's dangerous. It leads black women to believe that all black men who are successful only want a white woman. It also gives a jaw-dropping display of the angry black woman stereotype when she proceeds to set his car on fire with all his possessions inside.

Gloria Matthews is the pathetic character who finds love, but only after she fawns ridiculously over her gay ex-husband. She is the shining example of an overweight woman with low self-esteem who believes she doesn't deserve better than a man who comes for a "hit it and quit it" visit every once in a while.

McMillan tries to redeem all of these two-dimensional characters by the end of the story, but she falls short because none of these women truly feels complete without a man. In fact, they are all trying to get just comfortable enough so that they can "exhale" when they finally meet Mr. Right.

While a lot of black women would be happy if they found a good man to share their life with, they are not holding their breath waiting for him to come along. It's the notion that women are always on guard, always waiting, that makes the prospect of a lifetime of "singledom" seem unbearable. This pervasive view undermines women's quest for independence because it makes many of us feel that without the love and support of a romantic partner, our lives are void of meaning and purpose. These pressures make us feel that we are toiling on a futile, selfish path that will lead to a financial gain but an emotional abyss.

Media imagery may play a role in why women feel compelled to get married, but religion has an equally powerful stronghold on this ideal.

One of the most commonly recited passages at weddings is I Corinthians 13:4–8:

> Love is patient and kind; love is not jealous or boastful;
> it is not arrogant or rude. Love does not insist on its own way; it
> is not irritable or resentful;
> it does not rejoice at wrong, but rejoices in the right.
> Love bears all things, believes all things, hopes all things,
> endures all things.
> Love never ends

It's unlikely that anyone will attend a Christian ceremony without hearing these words. The repetition sends an unconscious message to those listening that love, and its conduit marriage, are essential components to God's plan as it is written in Mark 10:6–9:

> But from the beginning of creation, "God made them male
> and female."
> "For this reason a man shall leave his father and mother and be
> joined to his wife,
> and the two shall become one flesh." So they are no longer two
> but one flesh.
> What therefore God has joined together, let not man put asunder.

What could be a greater goal for a person of faith than finding the one you are meant to be with? Then again, the key line that believers should pay attention to is "God joined together." Perhaps singles and those who judge them should consider that they simply haven't met the person selected for them by the Divine Father.

Of course there are those who argue that marriage or a spiritual connection with another has become less important in the black community because too many black men are involved with someone of a different race. Black women have been led to believe that interracial marriage is why they aren't getting married to black men. To hear it told or to look at the big screen, you'd think that blacks are the minority with the highest percentage of interracial marriages.

The truth is that according to the 2000 census, only 7 percent of all African Americans married outside of their race, compared with more than half of Native Americans, 14 percent of Hispanics and 16 percent of Asians. *Black Enterprise* magazine, citing Renee Romano, author of *Race Mixing: Black and White Marriages in Post War America*, discusses African Americans' "reluctance to marry across racial lines" resulting from a combination of pride, identity, and white racism. In fact, Romano claims that between 65 and 85 percent of African Americans marry each other regardless of education level.[1]

What this means is that we can't blame white women for taking black men, nor can we say that television, movies, or black women are each solely to blame for the disintegration of the African American family. We do know that the answer as to why increasing numbers of black women are single is complicated, and the answer requires more than dredging up outdated, incorrect, and ineffective expectations and assumptions.

African American women may not know all the reasons that they are single in greater numbers, but they are proving they are prepared to deal with that reality. In doing so, they are doing their best to combat these myths and carve out lives that are full, happy, and anything but lonely.

20

Salvation for Single Sistahs?

Is Marriage All It's Cracked Up to Be?

The question has to be asked: is the only salvation for single sistahs to live out their lives solo, successful, and certainly not lonely, but accepting that any distant aspiration for a man, a partner, may never be fulfilled? If the answer is yes, then the future for these women doesn't look so bad. After all, what they lack from a man they have attained through friends, family, faith, and fulfilling careers.

But a vast majority of people suggest that the alternative is for women not to linger in their singlehood; they should pound the pavement for a man instead of seeking comfort and fulfillment in their friends and family. In doing so, they will be able to cultivate a life that will allow them to accept whoever steps into their worlds promising that elusive "happily ever after."

Some well-meaning people propose that black women flock to online dating. According to Jupiter Research, an Internet consultancy, the online dating market now has revenue of more 700 million dollars. And it estimates that more than 20 million people frequent online dating sites every month.[1] With so many available people out there in cyberspace on sites like True.com, Match.com, Yahoo! Personals, and so on, it would seem that logging on would increase the odds of finding a man.

But while the likelihood of meeting men may increase, there is still no guarantee they'll be the right men.

One potential hazard of online sites is the possible risk of being exposed to a criminal — most of these sites do not conduct background checks on individuals who post a profile. "There are no authoritative national statistics on serious crimes arising from online dating, but such cases periodically make headlines. A couple of examples: A Philadelphia man, Jeffrey Marsalis, was accused of raping several women he met through Match.com, and was sentenced in October to ten years in prison. A Cleveland firefighter, George Greer, was indicted last June for raping a woman he met through an internet dating site," cites a 2008 AP article.[2]

While you might not meet a rapist online, you could very well meet someone who is extremely disturbed or a guy who is just out to see how many women he can pick up. It's true that in day-to-day life you don't generally screen your dates either. You do, however, have the option of seeing where they work, meeting their friends, and getting a vibe from them before even agreeing to go out; that's something the Web doesn't allow.

Black women could also just bite the bullet and settle. Lori Gottlieb, author of the *Atlantic Monthly* article "Marry Him!" says that, despite their success and ambition, every woman feels a sense of dread if she reaches the age of thirty and isn't married. Her solution for this overwhelming sense of dread coupled with regret is to settle for whatever man you can get. She says that while this may seem to be an "enormous act of resignation," once a woman does it, she more than likely finds she's content. Gottlieb says she knows "it's not politically correct to get behind settling — it's downright un-American! Our culture tells us to keep our eyes on the prize (while our mothers, who know better, tell us not to be so picky), and the theme of holding out for true love (whatever that is — look at the divorce rate) permeates our collective mentality." She says if you think that picking your husband because you are madly in love with him ensures that you won't find a way to complain about him—just like you would for "Mr. Good Enough," whom you have settled for—you are wrong. Gottlieb says her married friends often claim to envy her single life, saying, among other things, that she is lucky because she gets to have sex with whomever she wants. She responds that if someone really believes that she's so fortunate, that woman should send her husband to Gottlieb. Of course, she remarks, no one ever obliges, seemingly pointing out that the women don't truly believe that being unmarried is all that wonderful.[3]

What Gottlieb fails to consider is that while these women are living lives that may be safe, they are unfulfilling, which is one of the leading causes cited for infidelity. People who no longer felt connected to their mate seek affection elsewhere. Gottlieb also doesn't address what happens to these marriages once the children leave home. If the reason a lot of these women settle for a man who is good enough rather than someone they are thrilled with is to have kids, when those children becomes adults what connection remains between the two people? I would argue that starting a marriage on a foundation that isn't built on love, respect, and devotion gives way to a union that has very little chance of survival. It would seem that her arguments for marriage are as outdated as the institution of marriage itself.

Settling for love without commitment is a path that a lot of African American women take. Cohabitation has reached an all-time high in this country, while the marriage rate has sunk to new lows. It makes one wonder if living with someone is a viable alternative to marriage if it means that you won't have to grow old without a man in your life. Yet it would seem that this option doesn't necessarily deliver the security and faithfulness that are supposed to follow wedding vows. One famous example is Sean "P. Diddy" Combs's relationship with Kim Porter. In an *Essence* magazine article, "No Ordinary Love," a pregnant Porter spoke glowingly about her on-again, off-again romance with hip-hop mogul Combs. The unmarried mother said she understood how his business life often interfered with their home life, and that it was something she was willing to tolerate. "As long as he makes us feel like a family, I'm fine. There'll be one day when he won't be working so hard, and then we will have a lifetime."[4]

Unfortunately, their lifetime together wasn't meant to be. Porter, who now has three children with Combs and one from a previous relationship, left Combs a few months after the article was published. She had told *Essence* that if her former boyfriend of twelve years was to propose to her, "I would say no, not because I don't want to get married, but because he's not ready to get married. When I get married, I want to stay married. I want both parties to be on the same page at the same time, and to leave a certain type of behavior behind. That's a commitment I don't think he's ready for."[5]

However, Porter didn't need to guess whether or not Combs was ready to be a husband. Back in that December article he said, "It's not a reflection on how much I love Kim. It's just I'm learning to be a good boyfriend. When I'm finished with this step, I'll move on to the next step."[6] Sadly, he didn't learn to take that step. He left her for a two-year relationship with singer Jennifer Lopez in 1998. After they were back together, he further humiliated her by getting another woman pregnant close to the same time they did the 2006 interview together—just short of the birth of his twin girls. Ironically, even after their split Porter remains dedicated to him, refusing to attack him or his character, once again demonstrating the loyalty and resilience of black women. Her story also shows the downside of creating a family with a man who has no sincere interest in being a family man. You run the risk of ending up a single mother trying to raise children who respect women and respect the institution of marriage while you are still looking for a man with whom you can share your life.

Any of these man-catching methods presumes that marriage is a more stable, healthier, happier lifestyle than being single—that it is an institution that ensures a life without loneliness. However, a 2005 survey, "The Consequences of Marriage for African Americans," by the Institute for American Values, seems to contradict these notions.

Of the ten major findings from this report, three jump off the page. The first is that black women seem to benefit from marriage significantly less than white women do. Second, the study found that, on average, unions between whites appear to be filled with more happiness and less strife than those of African Americans. Finally, but more important, black women seem to benefit less from marriage than black men in terms of family life and physical health, often being in inferior health than single black women.[7]

This is not to say that marriage doesn't afford some benefits. The study found some upsides, as well. Marriage seems to provide more of a financial benefit to blacks versus whites. In fact, married black families are far less likely to live in poverty than other African American families. Also, black children with married parents have fewer behavioral problems, better self-esteem, tend to put off having sex longer, and do slightly better in school. Additionally, growing up with a dad in the home, especially one who is married to the mother, can dramatically improve the outcomes for young black males.[8]

Yet, to get all of these benefits from marriage, the union between the two parents must be strong, positive, and consistent; meaning the parents must remain together throughout the child's life. Otherwise the gains are quickly lost when the children find themselves the product of a broken home.

Black women have to weigh whether the pluses associated with marriage are truly enough for them to beat themselves up about being single, causing them to not enjoy the present because they are focused on what could be. As statistics show, the myths associated with marriage—

including the one that says women live longer and are happier with a spouse—aren't true for black women. Given that, choosing to remain single could ultimately be the wiser choice.

Companionship is desired by most people, but a husband isn't the only person who can provide it. A lot of women have defined their own family through a collection of friends, colleagues, church members, and so on. Others take refuge in themselves, being their own best friend and support, never lonely, never longing, just accepting the gifts they've been given. As black women, we should know that our girlfriends can be there for some things, but they can't be everything, so learning to be there for yourself is crucial.

African American women who can't fathom navigating this life on their own can seek out a man, any man, to be by their side. But it needs to be said that simply having a man can't give a woman the peace, stability, and the assurances they are looking for. Joy comes from within. Without liking who you are, there's very little chance that someone else will like you.

Ultimately women have to save themselves and not define who they are through the eyes of a man. When he's gone, either through death or decision, what becomes of you then? True salvation from a life of loneliness comes when you know who you are, what you want, and accept that even though you may not get everything you thought you would, what you do have is enough to sustain you.

21

Lone Warriors

Single Black Women Fight for a Brighter Future

If we rely solely on the statistics, the prospect of single black women getting married is infinitesimal. Yet most of them, including a lot of the women featured in this work, believe that their present and future happiness is not rooted solely in finding a man to wed. It's true that many would welcome the opportunity to grow old with someone; it is also accurate to say that all lone warriors forging forward in lieu of this are carving out fulfilling and blissful lives. They are doing so by excelling in their careers and surrounding themselves with love from family and friends. They are trusting in their faith. They are getting to know themselves so they are a complete and well-adjusted individual should a fitting partner come along. They are sharing their stories with the world so that other women know that being single means your life is not devoid of love or filled with loneliness.

Historically speaking, it's very clear when and how black women became the sole support and driving force behind the majority of African American families and themselves. Following the era of slavery and the Civil War, black men were gainfully employed, often making them the breadwinners of their families. However, when European immigration picked up, these same men frequently found their jobs dispersed to others. With limited money or opportunity for employment, a lot of black families were forced to accept public assistance. As explained in an article in *Essence* by Susan Taylor, "In the 1970s, the welfare system forced the separation of financially strapped inner-city parents by instituting the 'no man in the household rule'; that's when the number of families headed by Black single mothers increased by about 257 percent."[1]

It is obvious that outside forces have long conspired to thwart the growth and maintenance of the African American family, but what's less clear is why black men have lost the fight to recapture their women and their families as they did during times of slavery and war. Perhaps their spirit has been broken by centuries of oppression, or possibly the lack of strong role models has left them without the skills to regain what's been lost. Whatever the cause, the ramifications have been generations of black men behind bars, unemployed, and dying at young ages.

The situation has also led to apathy on the part of many black women when it comes to black men having a major role in their lives and the lives of their children. They were forced to seek out new ways to build a solid foundation for themselves and in some cases their children. While they've accepted the fact that they are and will be alone, most do not believe this means they have to settle for a life that is less satisfying or stable than one they would have with a man. Indeed, the quest for motherhood has guided some to have children without a constant male presence and the financial support they would provide.

President Barack Obama addressed this issue in a speech at Trinity United Church on the South Side of Chicago on Father's Day in 2008. He said, "Too many fathers are MIA. Too many fathers are AWOL." Drawing on his own experience of being abandoned at the age of two by his father, he said, "There's a hole in your heart if you don't have a male figure in the home that can guide you and lead you and set a good example for you."[2]

Actor Hill Harper has made it his mission to inspire black youth to be responsible young men and women and to seek out and maintain relationships that enhance their self-esteem and strengthen the African American community. His newest title, *Letters to a Young Sister: DeFINE Your Destiny*, targets young African American women and encourages them to know their self-worth so that they will not succumb to situations that keep them from reaching their potential. Harper says he wrote the books to counter the images created and projected by his profession, which has damaged the psyche of black youth. "The entertainment business is decimating the esteem of our young people more than any other people." He continued that "we need to fight against the influences that are making our young men's self-worth inexplicably linked to rims on cars, or our young women feel they aren't worthy of love unless they dress in certain ways."[3]

It's easy to see where young black boys get the idea that gaudy materialism is something to emulate. Shows such as MTV's *Cribs* and *Pimp My Ride* display the riches that come with success; however, they fail to show the hard work and dedication required to achieve these items. And programs like *I Love New York* and *College Hill* don't provide a better example to young black women on how to dress and behave. Unfortunately there seems to be an endless stream of these shows, which continues to stoke these harmful ideals in African American children.

If there are few to no images that set a proper example for young blacks, where are they supposed to learn about behavior, love, and relationship longevity? The best place would be at home, but with the state of the black family such as it is, the next option may be from the example of African Americans in the spotlight. Black men can look for guidance from President Barack Obama and actor Hill Harper, among others. Whereas African American women can follow the lead of scores of females like Susan L. Taylor, actress Ruby Dee, Dr. Julianne Malveaux, Tyra Banks, and Oprah Winfrey, who through their words and actions are proving that black women can fashion respectable, gratifying lives with or without a man.

In one of her last "In the Spirit" columns as editorial director of *Essence* magazine, Susan L. Taylor discusses how African American women can revive the black family by seeking marriage. She recounts her successful tales as a matchmaker that led to the formation of several new black families. She follows by saying, "Nothing is more thrilling than being in love. But for black folks, the most unwed people in the nation, a partnership is an even higher calling."[4]

Taylor says that "black love is our strength, the glue that holds families and communities together, the means to secure our children, build wealth and end the state of emergency that we are in." Her plan for reversing this cultural trend that has left black women alone and fighting for the survival of the race is to implore African Americans to be "strategic and proactive. Taylor issues a call to arms for black women; an edict to them to plot a better future for themselves by offering black men understanding, forgiveness, and releasing them from blame. What she fails to mention is what black men will offer to women to ensure their happiness.

Taylor goes on to cite an impassioned appeal by Brooklyn activist and author Kevin Powell during a gathering of black men at the Joint Center for Political and Economic Studies, at which he "cautioned Black men to move to higher moral ground by doing something central to the recovery of our community: Stop betraying Black women and supporting one another in infidelities." Taylor says women applauded, but she says we bear some responsibility for the state of black America, as well. She says, "We, too, have work to do. We must walk the path of forgiveness and heal any anger or resentment, which poisons relationships."

Basically she dredges up the "angry black woman" stereotype, holding it up as if it were universally true. While I am sure some African American women have been cross with their mates or are bitter about their single status, not all need to be told to turn the other cheek. In fact, even inadvertently perpetuating the idea that black women are hostile only serves to further distance us from one another. Perhaps black men and women need to have the positive traits of African American women reinforced instead of the negative images or clichés. Singer/songwriter Raheem DeVaughn does a brilliant job expressing why black-on-black love is important in the song "Woman":

> And even as a single parent momma you still hold it down
> some how (thank you momma)
> Making ends meet somehow (thank you momma)
> I appreciate your strength (thank you)
> How you never bite your lip to say what's on your mind (thank you)[5]

Even single black women like myself who come from stable, married two-parent homes find ourselves alone because a lot of the men we encounter need to be groomed to be a husband or are simply choosing not to marry. Despite this reality, the pressure and desire for African American women to be married remains. Interestingly Taylor makes the point to also tell women that they "may have to help *make* a husband."[6]

A lot of black women, especially those who have struggled to achieve professional success, make one thing abundantly clear: they are tired of constantly having to raise a grown man by helping him grasp his responsibility as a partner. Most say what they want is a man who comes to them with his act together, ready, willing, and able to be with them. Yet if African American females aren't willing to shoulder one more burden, which is to help our men regain their confidence and bear with them as they learn how to be a proper boyfriend, lover, then husband, how will things ever change?

If they don't want the extra work of shaping a man, women might consider taking heed of the example being set by Dr. Julianne Malveaux, Tyra Banks, and Oprah Winfrey; all of whom are at the pinnacle of success in their career and are, by all appearances, happily unmarried. They take pleasure in their single lives without lamenting the fact that they aren't wearing a ring.

Dr. Julianne Malveaux is an economics expert who demonstrates that education can be the key to freedom from a relationship of necessity. As the head of Bennett College for Women, a historically black college, she has spent decades shaping the minds of African American women.

Then there is former supermodel Tyra Banks, who owns her own production company and hosts several hit shows. She is the epitome of beauty, fame, and fortune who thus far isn't rushing to get to the altar. Instead she's seemingly turning her attention to building her television empire while pushing her audiences, which are mostly comprised of women, to accept themselves and to fight against societal stereotypes and expectations.

Finally, there is media mogul Oprah Winfrey, who, despite being in a long-term relationship, continues to show women that marriage is not the right choice for everyone. Through her philanthropic work, which includes building a girl's leadership academy in South Africa, Winfrey continues to persuade women to follow their dreams, try to find their own joy, and not let a relationship define them.

Of course, none of these women advocate a life of solitude. Their point is simply that not getting married does not have to be the criteria by which you are judged.

Still, there will always be people like Taylor who suggest that in addition to adjusting attitudes about one another, blacks need to engage in a little old-fashioned matchmaking. "Help hook people up! Introduce emotionally healthy single folks who you think might make a match."

She says that "these are the greatest blessings we can give to our family, our friends, and our beloved community."

The crucial part of the sentence is the phrase "emotionally healthy." For decades now, the emotional fabric of the black community has been damaged by the reality that more than two-thirds of black girls are raised solely by their mothers. It begs the question: how can these same young women have positive relationships with men when they have limited exposure to them in their lives and homes? The lack of male influence coupled with the romantic notion that a man is supposed to be a stable force that will rescue them makes it easy to see why most match-ups don't generally last.

Still, if you do happen to find someone to share your life with, there is no guarantee that you won't find yourself single again at some point. This is why it is so important to have your own identity and sense of self-worth. Take legendary actress Ruby Dee, for example. After being married to actor Ossie Davis nearly a half century, he passed away, leaving her alone. Despite this, she is the picture of strength, continuing to act and succeed in her chosen profession rather than retreating and allowing herself to wither away. Simply by continuing to live her life, she shows that whether you choose to marry or not, all women will find themselves single at multiple points in their lives. The key to getting through it without feeling alone is to have a positive self image and surround yourself with love.

Although it is an uphill battle, most of us have not given up on finding someone with whom we can share at least part of our lives. For me and most of the women in this book, wanting to marry is something that doesn't come from a fear of peer pressure or a need to conform. It comes from an internal, some might say God-given, pull that has heightened with age. Having said that, I have no need simply to be married; I am not in love with the concept of the institution of marriage. Rather, I'm enthralled with the idea that a person, one man, will inspire me to want to join my life with his, even if for a brief time.

However, this desire comes only after learning to love myself and learning what my needs are over the last few years when I was finally alone. You see, from the time I was fourteen years old until my thirty-third birthday, I was constantly involved with someone.

Over the years, the thought of being married occurred to me mostly because I felt like I was an odd ball, a standout but not in a good way. My parents met as teens, had three children, and are still together to this day. My younger brother had my nephew with his high school sweetheart, while my baby brother has also spent years with his high school girlfriend. I felt as if something was wrong with me because I failed to make it to the altar with anyone.

However, I've learned that being alone has been the best thing for me. I've done things I never thought I would do by myself, such as buying a home and a car, doing major house repairs, and becoming financially independent. In doing so I no longer question why I am not married; I thank God I haven't been yet. I know that when, or if, I do tie the knot, I will come into the union as a whole, happy, fulfilled individual that has something to share with another person. And, if I don't get married, I know I will be OK; still happy, still fulfilled, and still satisfied with all that I worked hard to accomplish and all the love I have in my life.

Ultimately I hope that all single black women learn to measure their lives not by whom they are or aren't with but by the things that really matter: the number of people whose lives they've touched and how they will be remembered. My ideal is reflected in the song "Seasons of Love from the play *Rent* by Jonathan Larson.

Five Hundred Twenty-Five Thousand Six Hundred Minutes.
How do you measure the life of a woman or a man?

The answer that Larson comes up with is that the proper way to measure someone's life is in love—by gauging someone's impact on those around them, the number of lives they touch, the people who missed them, and the joyful things they have inspired.

The song points out that love is not something shared only between a man and a woman; it's the gift we've been given to share with everyone and everything on the planet. So, instead of looking at the one specific kind of love I or other single women don't have, I challenge black women to fight to get through life alone and not lonely, concentrating on the love you have given, received, and shared.

NOTES

Part One Introduction

1. Bella DePaulo, *Singled Out: How Singles are Stereotyped, Stigmatized, and Ignored, and Still Live Happily Ever After* (New York: St. Martin's Press, 2006), p. 2.
2. Ibid., p. 247.
3. Ibid.

Chapter 3

1. DePaulo, *Singled Out*, p. 10.
2. Michael E. Ross, "Report Offers Grim Forecast for Young Black Men," *Newsweek*, Apr. 7, 2006.
3. Avis Thomas-Lest, "More Black Women Adopt New Path to Families," Washingtonpost.com, Feb. 10, 2003, p. B01; "More Black Women Adopting Solo," *Dallas Morning Star*, July 18, 2003.

Chapter 4

1. The Enjoli commercial can be seen on YouTube at http://www.youtube.com/watch?v=4X4MwbVf5OA.

2. Marianne Page and Anne Huff, "Divorce and Marriage Affect Black Children More," UC Davis News Service, May 25, 2005.

Chapter 6

1. William Raspberry, "Why Our Black Families Are Failing," *Washington Post*, July 25, 2005, p. A19.
2. Ibid.
3. Andrew Billingsley, *Climbing Jacobs Ladder: The Enduring Legacy of African-American Families* (New York: Simon & Schuster, 1994).
4. Maggie Gallagher, *The Abolition of Marriage* (Washington, D.C.: Regnery, 2007), p.120, citing Reynolds Forley, "After the Starting Line: Blacks and Women in an Uphill Pace," *Demography*, Nov. 1988, p. 487.
5. Raspberry, "Why Our Black Families Are Failing."
6. Ibid.

Chapter 7

1. Mariah Carey, Christopher "Tricky" Stewart, Crystal "Cri$tyle" Johnson, and Terius "the Dream" Nash, "Touch My Body," *E=MC2* (2008) Island Records.
2. The Neptunes (Hugo, Chad; Williams, Pharrell) "Milkshake" performed by Kelis, *Tasty* (2003) Arista.
3. Rosenbloom, "Taming of the Slur," *New York Times*, July 13, 2006.
4. March of Dimes.Com, Quick Reference Fact Sheets.

Chapter 8

1. Vanessa E. Jones, "The Angry Black Woman: Tart-Tongued or Driven and No-Nonsense, She Is a Stereotype That Amuses Some and Offends Others," Boston Globe, April 20, 2004.
2. Ibid.

3. Ibid.

4. Ibid.

5. HIV/AIDS Surveillance report, Vol. 18: Cases of HIV infection and AIDS in the United States, 2006, US Centers for Disease Control and Prevention, 2008.

6. African American HIV/AIDS Statistics, www.avert.org, April 8, 2008.

7. HIV/AIDS among women, CDC Fact Sheet, April 2006.

8. Associated Press, "'Could Mr. Right Be White?' More Black Women Consider 'Dating Out,'" www.CNN.com, August 6, 2007.

9. Ibid.

Chapter 9

1. Matthew Vasiliauskas, "Like Tea Falling From the Sky: A Profile of Effie Brown," www.FilmMonthly.com, December 11, 2005.

2. James C. Johnson, "Paving Her Way," *Black Enterprise Magazine*, July 2006.

3. Ibid.

4. Ibid.

5. Gail Marks Jarvis, "Racial Divide in Savings," *Chicago Tribune*, October 12, 2007.

Chapter 11

1. George Alexander VII, "Sheila Bridges Transforms Spaces; Award Winning Interior Designer Puts Her Signature on Client's Personal Surroundings," *Ebony Magazine*, November 11, 2007.

2. Ibid.

Chapter 12

1. CBS News Poll, "Poll: 20% in U.S. Caring for Aging Parents," February 19, 2007.

2. Jim Hopkins, "African American Women Step Up in the Business World: More Women of Color Take the Lead on the Path to Entrepreneurship," *USA Today*, August 25, 2006.

3. Center for Women's Business Research, "Number of Minority Women-Owned Business Expected to Reach 1.2 Million in 2002," December 18, 2001.

4. DePaulo, *Singled Out*, pp. 139, 140.

Chapter 13

1. www.BlackMilitaryWorld.com, "Study: Blacks, Hispanics, Women Most Satisfied with the Military," June 2008.

Chapter 14

1. Sperling's BestPlaces, "Going Solo in the USA."

2. Karen Cook, "Caregiver for Aging Parents: What's An 'Only Child' To Do," *Associated Content*, 2008.

Chapter 15

1. CBS News.com, "Marriage after 40? Not Possible?" May 31, 2006.

Chapter 17

1. Lori Gottlieb, "Marry Him: The Case for Settling for Mr. Good Enough," *Atlantic Monthly*, March 2008.

2. Ibid.

3. Ibid.

Chapter 18

1. DePaulo, *Singled Out*, p. 10.

2. Ibid.
3. Fantasia. "Baby Mama," *Free Yourself* (2005) J Records.
4. Menstuff.org/issues/byissue/infidelitystats.html, citing *USA Today*, December 21, 1998, based on a study by University of California, San Francisco.
5. LaShawn Daniels, Rodney Jerkins, Fred Jerkins III, Isaac Phillips, and Toni Estesher. "It's Not Right but It's Okay," *My Love Is Your Love* (1999) Arista.
6. Scott Storch and Robert Waller. "Me, Myself and I," *Dangerously in Love* (2003) Columbia.
7. Shep Crawford and Tamia. "Me," *Between Friends* (2007) Image/Gallo.
8. Jordin Sparks and J. Fauntleroy II, Eric "Blue Tooth" Griggs, H. Mason Jr., D. Thomas, and S. Russell. "No Air," *Jordin Sparks* (2008) 19, Jive, Zomba.

Chapter 19

1. *Black Enterprise Magazine*, "Mixed Marriage: Blacks Are Less Likely Than Other Ethnicities to Marry Interracially," June 2008.

Chapter 20

1. David Crary, "Online Dating Industry Split on Background Check Issue," Associated Press, February 12, 2008.
2. Ibid.
3. Gottlieb, "Marry Him!"
4. Jeannine Amber, "No Ordinary Love," *Essence*, December 2006.
5. Ibid.
6. Ibid.
7. Institute for American Values, "The Consequences of Marriage for African Americans: A Comprehensive Literature Review," 2005.
8. Ibid.

Chapter 21

1. Susan L. Taylor, "Let's Get Married!" *Essence*, March 2008.
2. Michael McAuliff, "Barack Obama, Speaking in Church, Urges Fathers to Set Examples," *New York Daily News*, June 16, 2008.
3. Joyce E. Davis, "Brother to Sister," *Upscale*, July 2008.
4. Taylor, "Let's Get Married!"
5. Raheem DeVaughn. "Woman," *Love Behind the Melody* (2008) Jive.
6. Taylor, "Let's Get Married!"

About the Author

MTamanika (Nika) C. Beamon is an African American female currently residing
in New Jersey.

In her fifteen years as a journalist,
she's worked at various television stations
including WABU-TV in Boston, ESPN
Classic, and WABC-TV in New York.
She also served as coordinating producer
for *Like It Is with Gil Noble*, the country's longest-running African American
public affairs show. She has won several
awards including a Peabody Award for
ABC News' coverage of the September 11 attacks.

In 2000, she published her first novel, *Dark Recesses*, listed in *Inside
Magazine*'s Hidden Hit List column as a best-selling print on demand
title. In 2002, she completed her second novel, *Eyewitness*.

She is a member of the Writers Guild of America East and the
National Association of Black Journalists.

Not All Black Girls Know How to Eat

A Story of Bulimia

Stephanie Covington Armstrong

978-1-55652-786-9
$16.95 (CAN $18.95)

In this insightful and moving first-person narrative, Armstrong describes her struggle as a black woman with a disorder that is consistently portrayed as a white woman's problem. She traces her background and the factors that caused her behavior, some similar to but many very different from the causes of eating disorders in white women. In continual movement, from Los Angeles to New York to Vermont to London and back to California, Stephanie tries to escape her self-hatred and her food obsession by never slowing down, unaware that she is caught in downward spiral emotionally and spiritually as well as physically. Finally she can no longer deny that she will die if she doesn't get help, overcome her shame, and conquer her addiction to using food as a weapon against herself. But seeking help often reinforces rather than resolves her negative self-image, as she discovers her race makes her an oddity in the all-white programs for eating disorders. Her experiences answer many questions about why black women often do not seek traditional therapy for emotional problems.

Not All Black Girls Know How to Eat is an important book that breaks the silence and the stereotypes, getting the message out to women who do not fit media images: they are not alone. They can get help, learn to accept and love themselves, and even shatter some barriers in the process.

Financial Intimacy
How to Create a Healthy Relationship with Your Money and Your Mate

Jacquette M. Timmons

978-1-55652-775-3
$14.95 (CAN $16.95)

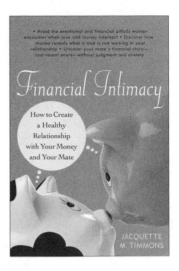

"Jacquette Timmons merges the practical with the political in her exciting work: not only does she give us great insight on our financial lives, she does the creative work of showing how our personal lives affect and interact with our resources and vice versa. A true contribution from a wise, compassionate, and perceptive guide." —Naomi Wolf, author of *The End of America: Letter of Warning to a Young Patriot* and *Give Me Liberty: A Handbook for American Revolutionaries*

There is a commonly held perception that we don't talk about money. Actually, we talk about it all the time—we are just having the wrong conversation.

In *Financial Intimacy* national investment expert and financial coach Jacquette M. Timmons addresses common financial issues that arise in relationships and encourages women to turn to their attention to their own relationship with money in order to provide a framework for asking questions and exchanging information that will allow both partners to know and understand each other's personal financial stories. In the process, couples will tap into emotions they might not be accustomed to expressing and will learn each other's financial preferences, prejudices, and tolerances and how to create a paradigm for living wealthy and well—in good times and bad.

Financial Intimacy elevates the conversation about money and gives women the tools to take the lead.

A Healing Grove

African Tree Remedies and Rituals for the Body and Spirit,

Stephanie Rose Covington

978-1-55652-764-7
$18.95 (CAN $20.95)

Reclaiming traditions based on plants and herbs has never been more important than it is today. Widespread use of chemicals, hormones, and additives introduce unknown substances into our bodies. On a larger scale, our future on the planet depends on our ability and willingness to incorporate earth-friendly practices into daily life. Where better to look for natural remedies and soothing rituals than Africa? It is, after all, the Mother Continent, allegedly the birthplace of the entire human race, and the keeper of ancient earth knowledge.

No newcomer to these traditions, Stephanie Rose Bird explores the practical uses, spiritual traditions, and historical aspects of trees in the heritage of African Americans and offers ways to rediscover and implement natural practices in twenty-first-century daily life. Bird intimately shares how trees have provided her with personal healing and explains how we can do the same. The topics covered are as diverse as a wood should be, including everything from hunting, gathering, and processing to natural divination, animal omens, oracles, signs, and forest medicine for wellness and beauty. *The Healing Grove* will lead not only to personal healing but to a lifestyle that will help heal our earth.